Spiritual Espresso
Volume I

Devotionals from *Strength for Today*

ISBN: 978-0-578-03725-7

All Scripture quotations are from the King James Bible 1611.

Visit our website at:
www.oldpathsjournal.com
www.domelleministries.com

For more copies write to:
Allen Domelle Ministries
PO Box 19
Inwood, WV 25428
or call (304) 839-9531

Table of Contents

No Fear, No Commandments

Deuteronomy 5:29
"O that there were such an heart in them, that they would fear me, and keep all my commandments always, that it might be well with them, and with their children for ever!"

Moses is reviewing with the children of Israel what happened years prior in the wilderness when God came and met with them at the bottom of Mount Sinai. What a moment this must have been for the children of Israel. The magnitude of this moment brought a fear in the hearts of the people so much so that they requested of Moses to go alone and receive the commandments that God was trying to hand to them. At this request, God came and used this time to teach His people the importance of keeping this attitude at all times. God said that if they would keep His commandments that it would go well with them.

Now as we look at this verse, we notice that the first requirement for keeping the commandments of God is a fear of God. O how America needs to get back to having a fear of God. This fear of God is not a trembling of fear because we are afraid. This fear is a reverential respect for the power that God holds.

As I think of having a fear of something, I am reminded of times when I have worked with electricity. I certainly, and most people do as well, have a fear of working with electricity. The reason why we have a fear of electricity is because we know what electricity can do to us. As long as we keep that fear in mind when we work with it, then we can use electricity to do many wonderful things for us. In like manner if we keep the fear of what God's power can do to us, then we can use that power to accomplish many things for Him.

Secondly, we notice that with a fear of God comes the keeping of God's commandments. Having a right fear of God motivates us to keep His commandments, for we know what can happen to us if we do not keep His commandments. Without a fear of God we will never be successful in keeping the commandments of God.

Now are you having problems in keeping the commandments of God? If you are, then maybe what you ought to do is get a greater fear of God. Let me just remind you, God can take you down in a moments notice. The knowledge of this ought to cause you to have a fear of God. If you have no fear you can be guaranteed to fail at keeping His commandments.

Thirdly, we see the result of keeping the commandments of God is that things will go well for us in life. This does not mean that we will not have hard times. This means that life in general will go well for us. So the decision we must make today is this, are we going to keep God's commandments so it will go well for us or are we going to disobey the commandments of God, which will result in things not going well for us? I believe the obvious decision should be easy.

We must remember that it all starts out with a fear of God. If you will read God's Word, you will find that this fear will be placed in you by God Himself. Spend time reading God's Word so that you may obtain a fear of God. This will cause you to keep His commandments, and life in general will go well for you.

Principles Determine Our Loyalty

Deuteronomy 13:1-3
"If there arise among you a prophet, or a dreamer of dreams, and giveth thee a sign or a wonder, And the sign or the wonder come to pass, whereof he spake unto thee, saying, Let us go after other gods, which thou hast not known, and let us serve them; Thou shalt not hearken unto the words of that prophet, or that dreamer of dreams: for the LORD your God proveth you, to know whether ye love the LORD your God with all your heart and with all your soul."

It is important for every person to learn that principles must determine whether or not we are going to be loyal to someone who calls himself a man of God.

In the verses that we just read, we see God teaching His people how to determine whether or not they should follow someone who calls himself a prophet. God says that no matter what great sign a prophet gives or what great wonder a prophet may perform, if this prophet tells them to go after other gods, they should have nothing to do with this man. In fact, God says, that at times, He would allow this to happen to His people just to see how much they truly loved Him. God says He will know the love of His people towards Him by how they respond to a false prophet.

This same principle still applies to us today. In a world that is filled with television and radio preachers, we as God's people need to be very careful who we allow ourselves to be influenced by. The most important thing that we should determine is whether or not a man is preaching the truths of God correctly. It matters not how much truth this man may give, if one of his principles pulls us away from the truths of the Word of God then we should not listen to him, watch him or read his books. We must remember that we must always be loyal to principle before being loyal to a person or an institution.

Loyalty is a wonderful thing to have as long as loyalty is being kept in check by principle. What happens to many people is they become more loyal to a man than they do to principle. Then these same people will say they are doing right because they are being loyal. This is not always true. We are to be loyal first to the truths of God's Word. Then we are to be loyal to the man of God as long as he is loyal to the truths of God's Word. The very second that a man of God leaves God's truths is when we should stop being loyal to him.

God says that He will allow us to cross the paths of such individuals just to see how much we truly love Him. If we choose to be loyal to man over principles, then our love for God is not that great. Your love for God is tested by whom you choose to be loyal to. How is your love for God? Do you find yourself giving excuses as you listen to so-called preachers who preach messages full of doctrinal error? Be loyal to principles and you will never regret it in the long run.

Fortifying The Home

Deuteronomy 22:8
"When thou buildest a new house, then thou shalt make a battlement for thy roof, that thou bring not blood upon thine house, if any man fall from thence."

In the days when this scripture was written, God used the architecture of homes to teach a valuable lesson that we all must apply in order to keep our homes strong.

Many times the homes built in these days had a place on the roof where you could walk around. You may recall in the Bible that David, when he saw Bathsheba, was walking on his roof. This was not an uncommon thing as most houses were built so that you could walk on the roof. Now God warned the people that when they built a house in this fashion, they were to make a *"battlement"* for the roof. This word *"battlement"* means "a wall built for fortification." In other words, they were to build a wall on top of the house so that no one would fall to the ground and hurt themselves. Not only was this wall a protection from them falling, but it was also a protection from anyone coming into their house through the roof. This wall was of great importance for the safety of the home.

The Devil is after our homes. He throws every kind of dart he can at the home to destroy it. He knows that if the homes are destroyed then the nation is going to be destroyed as well. Never in the history of our country have we seen the attack against the home like we see today.

We must build some walls of protection in our homes to protect them from being destroyed. This means we should have rules by which our children should live. We should have rules by which mom and dad should live so they do not destroy their marriage. We should have rules for parents and children to live by so that their home is protected from any outside enemy that would try to destroy the home. O how we

11

need to be careful to protect our homes. If needs be, being a little overboard is better than not enough. I would rather be safe than sorry. If we do not fortify our homes by establishing some rules by which to live, then we will find our homes in ruin and, oh, the heartache this will bring.

Don't be guilty of being shamed into letting down the rules. Don't be guilty of getting tired of fighting for the rules of your home. Always remember that those rules that you have established are there to protect your marriage, children and home. Those rules are there as a battlement to your house.

Personal Responsibility

Deuteronomy 24:16
"The fathers shall not be put to death for the children, neither shall the children be put to death for the fathers: every man shall be put to death for his own sin."

As God gave out the different regulations by which He expected His people to live, God gave a command to each individual that they were responsible for their own sin. God did not want to give a crutch to people to blame their sins on someone else. God wanted His people to take personal responsibility for their own actions. God went further in this teaching and commanded that no child should bear the punishment of sin because of what their parents have done and neither should the parents be held accountable for what their children have done. Every person was to be responsible for their own actions.

How much this teaching is needed today! As you listen to the court systems of our day and hear the defense of many of the defendants, what a shame that we try to blame everyone else for what we have done. The modern politically correct society that we live in today tries to blame those from the past for the actions of those who are alive today. How absurd this is for people to blame someone who did not force them to make their decision. Until we come to the point in our society when people start taking personal responsibility for their own actions, our society will never start recovering from the shambles that it is in today.

Most people know that the first step to recovering from anything is taking personal responsibility for their actions. Your parents did not make you do wrong. Though they may have led you down the wrong path in your life, you are the one that makes the choices for your own life and are responsible for your own actions. No relative, preacher, leader or group of people is responsible for your actions; you alone are responsible for your actions.

What even seems more absurd is in Christianity we try to give people an out for their actions by saying some evil spirit caused a person to do something. There are those in Christianity who will say that a person has a spirit of bitterness, or a spirit of anger, or a spirit of jealousy and so on. The whole reason they try to do this is to take the responsibility off of the person who is bitter or jealous. No, the whole reason a person is that way is because they choose to be that way. Nobody can make you do wrong! You choose what you do, and you must live with the consequences of your own actions.

Let each of us become a person who takes personal responsibility for our actions so that we can better face our problems. Until we take personal responsibility we will never overcome our shortcomings in life. By taking personal responsibility, we can overcome our shortcomings in life.

Preparing Followers For Your Vacancy

Deuteronomy 31:6
"Be strong and of a good courage, fear not, nor be afraid of them: for the LORD thy God, he it is that doth go with thee; he will not fail thee, nor forsake thee."

Moses is in the final days of his life as we read this thirty-first chapter of Deuteronomy. In the verse that we just read, Moses is challenging Joshua and the people to be strong and to have good courage. They knew that he was about to die and I can only imagine the fear that these people faced as they wondered what they were going to do without their great leader. Moses challenged these people to be strong and have good courage in his absence. He reminded them that the same God that he served would still be there for them when he is gone. What Moses was doing was preparing the people for what they were to do once he was gone.

Every leader must first of all realize that they are not going to live forever. Every follower must realize that their leader is only human and that they are not going to live forever. Not facing this is not facing reality. One day, if you are a leader, you will die. So if what you are leading is ever going to keep on going, then you must prepare your followers for your vacancy after your death.

Great leadership always prepares their followers for what they are supposed to do once they are gone. Our Saviour, Jesus Christ, did this with His disciples. As you read the Gospels you see Jesus constantly telling His disciples that He is going to be gone someday and when He is gone He taught them what they were supposed to do in His absence. This is what great leadership will do. If you are a leader you must prepare those who follow you on how to carry on once you are gone. As leaders we must remind our followers, that the God we serve will still be alive and well, though we are gone. God will not leave them just because you are gone. As a leader you must remind them of this. Not only must you remind them of this, but you must also train them to do what you are doing so that what you are doing will go on after you are gone. In doing so, the work that we have spent our lives doing can go forward and continue even after our deaths.

Every leader must learn this valuable lesson. Whether you are a parent, pastor, business man or some other type of leader, you must prepare those whom you lead to do what you do all the time. This is why you are a leader. If you never train others to do what you are doing, then you are a poor leader. We never know when we will be gone, so we must spend our lives as leaders training those who follow us to do what we are doing. Leaders, if you were to die today, would your work be able to go on because you have trained someone else to take your place in your absence. If not, then start today training others to take your place. This is what great leaders do!

Every Decision Is Important

Joshua 9:14
"And the men took of their victuals, and asked not counsel at the mouth of the LORD."

We have in this verse the story of Joshua and the Gibeonites. The people of Gibeon had heard of the victories of the children of Israel, and fear had gripped their hearts about what they had seen happen to cities much mightier than they. So they came up with a plan, this plan was to get some old moldy bread and some worn out clothes and come to Joshua and the children of Israel and appear as if they came from a far country. In so doing, their goal was to make a league, or a treaty, as we would call it, with the Israelites thus saving their own lives. So they did just this and as they appeared to the children of Israel, Israel just took for granted that these people were telling the truth. The verse that we just read said they made this league with the Gibeonites without asking counsel of God. What a tragedy this was for these people who knew better. Because of this, they now would have to share part of their land with a people that God had intended for them not to share it with. All of this happened because they treated this decision as if it was not important.

Each of us can learn from this story the importance of making decisions and the importance of every decision. I do not know of a decision that is not important. If we all are just one decision away from ruining our life or from hurting our life, then I would think that every decision is important. Because every decision is important, then every decision should be bathed in prayer seeking the counsel of God as to what we should do with each decision that we face.

We should never go into a decision without spending time in prayer. We should never make a decision without spending time finding what the Bible says about this decision that we are about to make. Each and every decision is important, and we should never get so comfortable in making

17

decisions that we do not ask counsel of God about what we should do. The day we become this comfortable with our decisions is the day when we will find ourselves making some very foolish decisions.

Every one of us who has ever made a bad decision can always trace it back to the fact that we did not treat the decision with enough importance. Because of our lack of making the decision important, we already have faced the pain of making wrong decisions. Let us be careful in every decision that we make from now on. Let us face every decision as if it is a life and death decision. Let us not be quick in making decisions. Let us get counsel from God in every decision, for He must be a part of every decision we make.

The Importance Of The Altar

Joshua 22:26-27
"Therefore we said, Let us now prepare to build us an altar, not for burnt offering, nor for sacrifice: But that it may be a witness between us, and you, and our generations after us, that we might do the service of the LORD before him with our burnt offerings, and with our sacrifices, and with our peace offerings; that your children may not say to our children in time to come, Ye have no part in the LORD."

The two and a half tribes of Israel are now about ready to go back over to the land of their inheritance that they had been given by Moses. As they came to the Jordan River, they decided that they were going to build an altar. This altar was not about them getting right with God, but more importantly, this altar was about them staying right with God. You see, they knew that the Jordan River would become a border between them and the other tribes on the other side of the Jordan. They wanted to build this altar so that both sides would remember that they were a part of Israel and that they would never be denied the opportunity to cross over the Jordan River to go and sacrifice to their God. This altar was not only a memorial of what God had done in the past, but this altar was raised up to keep them right with God.

How interesting it is that the altar was being set up to keep them right with God and not for them to get right with God. Yes, the altar is about keeping us right with God. If a person will use the altar on a regular basis, then a person will find themselves staying right with God.

Far too many times we think the only reason why we use an altar at the church is so that we can get right with God, but this verse shows us another reason why we use the altar. The altar is a place to remember decisions we have made with God. When hearing the preaching of the Word of God, we should make decisions about things we are going to do and things we are not going to do. The altar is the place where we seal those decisions so that every time we go to church and see the altar, we are reminded of those decisions. Thus, in essence, the altar becomes a place of remembering decisions and also a place that keeps us right with God.

Let us all use the altar regularly so that in days to come and generations to come our decisions will be remembered. Let us not be guilty of being a people who never use the altar. You will find that those who never use the altar are usually people who have a harder time staying right with God. The altar is important! It is important because it is a place where we get right with God, but it is also a place where we stay right with God and a place that reminds us of the decisions we have made in the past.

A Good Formula For Success

Judges 6:14-16
"And the LORD looked upon him, and said, Go in this thy might, and thou shalt save Israel from the hand of the Midianites: have not I sent thee? And he said unto him, Oh my Lord, wherewith shall I save Israel? behold, my family is poor in Manasseh, and I am the least in my father's house. And the LORD said unto him, Surely I will be with thee, and thou shalt smite the Midianites as one man."

These verses come from the calling of Gideon as God reveals to Gideon that he is to deliver Israel from the hand of the Midianites. We see in the story of Gideon that instead of fighting for their food, they were hiding it. As God called Gideon, He called him a *"mighty man of valour."* What a compliment for God to give Gideon this title.

I must remind you, as I always remind people, the characters of the Bible all had the same fears and worries that we have today. The Midianite army was a huge army that no one had been able to conquer. On top of this, the children of Israel were afraid of these people. Yet, when we come to these verses, we see that God gave Gideon a formula for success. This formula will certainly help us today to be successful in the endeavors that we pursue.

First of all, we see that in order to be successful you must have the right strength. You will notice that God tells Gideon in verse 14 to go in the might that he has. Way too many times we are waiting for God to give us the strength to do something great for Him when God has already given us the strength we need. You may wonder, what is the right strength to be able to do the task that God wants you to do? That strength is the strength that you presently have. God wants you to step out on your strength, and as you step out on your strength, God will step in and give you more strength as you serve Him. Stop waiting for the strength, and just step out by faith with the strength that you presently have.

21

Secondly, in order to be successful you must have the right attitude. Notice the attitude of Gideon. He did not feel worthy to be used in such a great way. This is the right attitude and one that every Christian should have. God can use people who have a humble spirit. God cannot use in a great way those who believe God is honored to have them. Success is highly dependant upon the right attitude. Not only should you have an attitude of humility, but also I believe you should have a positive attitude and believe that God can use you. Yes, you should be humbled that God would use you, but you should also believe that God will use you.

Thirdly, in order to be successful you must have the right companion. Now who is the right companion in order to be successful? That companion would be God. As Romans 8:31 says, *"...If God be for us, who can be against us?"* When God is on your side you need not fear, for you have the right companion. But let me also expound even further and say that not only must God be your companion in all endeavors, but also your other companions must be right to keep you from failure.

So the three things we learned that are necessary for success are the right strength, the right attitude and the right companions. Without these you will never find success in your life.

Sin Is Ugly No Matter How You Paint It

Judges 17:3-4
"And when he had restored the eleven hundred shekels of silver to his mother, his mother said, I had wholly dedicated the silver unto the LORD from my hand for my son, to make a graven image and a molten image: now therefore I will restore it unto thee. Yet he restored the money unto his mother; and his mother took two hundred shekels of silver, and gave them to the founder, who made thereof a graven image and a molten image: and they were in the house of Micah."

What a tragic story we find here in the seventeenth chapter of Judges. Here we find a young man by the name of Micah who had stolen eleven hundred shekels of silver from his own mother. I do not know how it all came about, but it seems as if his conscience had gotten the best of him, and he came to his mother and told his mother that he had the money for which she was looking. As he restores the money to his mother, we see that his mother told him that she was going to use this money, that she had dedicated to the LORD, for the purpose of making an idol to worship. Now how in the world can you justify wrong by trying to spiritualize the wrong that you are going to do? This is exactly what this lady was trying to do. She was trying to paint her sin in a pretty way by saying that she had dedicated this money to the LORD. No matter how she tried to paint this picture, making idols is a sin.

It does not matter how a person may try to paint their sin, sin is always going to be sin. No matter how you try to paint sin, sin is always going to be ugly. Many times people try to spiritualize the wrong that they are doing so that they can justify this wrong in their own conscience. Let me say, it matters not if you can paint wrong in such a way that you justify it with your conscience, wrong is still wrong and sin is still sin no matter how you paint it.

Giving your tithe money to another good cause and not giving it to the church is still wrong. Compromising what the

Bible teaches to see more people saved is wrong no matter how you do it. Letting up on your preaching and standards to have bigger numbers in the church, so you can influence more people, is still wrong. We could go on and on with illustrations of trying to paint sin in a pretty way. We must always remember that God is not impressed with our sin even if we paint it in a good way. In 1 Samuel 15:22 God says, *"...to obey is better than sacrifice, and to hearken than the fat of rams."* God desires obedience to His Word more than He desires anything else. If we are not careful, we will paint sin in such a way that it appeases our conscience to the point that we will do this wrong and in so doing we will anger God. No matter how you paint sin, sin is sin and sin will always be ugly.

Are there some things in your life that you have tried to spiritualize so you can justify doing it even though you know it is wrong? Let me simply remind you that sin has a price tag. No matter how you paint sin, sin will always bring heartache. Instead of trying to spiritualize your wrong, why don't you just do right and you will see the blessings of God.

Be Good To Everybody

Ruth 2:8-11
"Then said Boaz unto Ruth, Hearest thou not, my daughter? Go not to glean in another field, neither go from hence, but abide here fast by my maidens: Let thine eyes be on the field that they do reap, and go thou after them: have I not charged the young men that they shall not touch thee? and when thou art athirst, go unto the vessels, and drink of that which the young men have drawn. Then she fell on her face, and bowed herself to the ground, and said unto him, Why have I found grace in thine eyes, that thou shouldest take knowledge of me, seeing I am a stranger? And Boaz answered and said unto her, It hath fully been shewed me, all that thou hast done unto thy mother in law since the death of thine husband: and how thou hast left thy father and thy mother, and the land of thy nativity, and art come unto a people which thou knewest not heretofore."

A wonderful truth we find in these verses come from the life of Ruth. As we know the story well, Ruth was the daughter-in-law of Naomi. Naomi's husband and two sons died, and she was left alone. With nothing left to her name, she told her daughters-in-law to go back to their families and their gods. Though Naomi tried to get Ruth to go back, she would not leave her mother-in-law but instead decided to stay with her and take care of her. When they came back to the homeland of Naomi, she told Ruth to go and glean in the field of a wealthy relative whose name was Boaz. When Boaz came out to see his employees working, he saw this young lady out there gleaning from the leftover crops that the servants had left behind. After finding out that this was the daughter-in-law of Naomi, Boaz told his servants to leave her alone and to even leave a little more than they usually do because he had seen how she treated her mother-in-law. Ruth never knew that her treatment of Naomi would lead her to the lineage of Christ. Because she was good to everyone, she was blessed in a great way.

How we must learn ourselves to be sure that we are good to everyone with whom we come in contact. We just never know to whom we are being good. It may be we are being good to the next great preacher of our nation. It may be we are being good to a future employer who will take care of us for the rest of our lives. It may be we are being good to someone who will be a future leader in a nation. We never know with whom we are talking. Because of this we should just be good to everyone. Would it not be sad if we were not good to everyone we came in contact with and ended up hurting our own future? Yes, you may be having a bad day, but you can still be good to everyone.

Be careful with how you respond to people. Your sharp response just may cause them to remember who you are, and that person with whom you are sharp may be the one who God intended to help you somewhere down the line. It does not take much to be good to people. We must make it a daily habit to be good to everyone. We just never know to whom we are being good, and they just may be someone who will help us later on down the road.

Don't Be Satisfied

Psalm 17:14-15
"From men which are thy hand, O LORD, from men of the world, which have their portion in this life, and whose belly thou fillest with thy hid treasure: they are full of children, and leave the rest of their substance to their babes. As for me, I will behold thy face in righteousness: I shall be satisfied, when I awake, with thy likeness."

As the psalmist prays to God in this Psalm, we find him reasoning with God about the wicked people of the world and how they seem to be satisfied with what they have. He talks about men who seem to have everything in life. They seem to have hidden treasures that never seem to end. They seem to have a family with which they are fulfilled. They seem to have enough monetarily to do in life what they want to do and still have enough left over to give plenty to their children. As the psalmist talks of this, he seems to infer that these men are happy and satisfied with what they have.

Then we come to the psalmist himself. The psalmist, after talking about how the heathen are satisfied with possessions, says he will only be satisfied with one thing; being like Christ. He makes the statement, *"I shall be satisfied, when I awake, with thy likeness."* O what a statement the psalmist has made here. Only one thing in life would satisfy him; being like Christ. Money would not satisfy him, though we know he had money for the psalmist was King David. Possessions would not satisfy him, though he had all the possessions that a person could desire. Having full families with several children is not what satisfied him, though he even had that. The psalmist wanted only one thing in life; to be like God. He said until the day he awakes in the likeness of God, he will not be satisfied.

O how this ought to be the prayer of every Christian. How every Christian should not be satisfied with where they are in life until they are completely like Christ. Yes, we preach that we ought to be satisfied with what we have, but there is one area I believe we should never be satisfied with; how far we have gone spiritually. The day you become satisfied with your spiritual growth is the day you stop growing. The day you become satisfied with the heights of your spirituality is the day you stop reaching new heights. We should every day have a hunger to be more like Christ. We should never be satisfied until we awake in His likeness.

Are you satisfied with your life? If you are, then can you honestly say you are like Christ? If you are not like Christ, then you should never be satisfied until you awake in His likeness. Let us, Christians, always be dissatisfied with our spirituality until we awake in the likeness of Christ.

Your History Does Not Determine Your Blessings

1 Samuel 2:30
"Wherefore the LORD God of Israel saith, I said indeed that thy house, and the house of thy father, should walk before me for ever: but now the LORD saith, Be it far from me; for them that honour me I will honour, and they that despise me shall be lightly esteemed."

The man of God, Eli, is now getting old, and his sons are in line to take over the office of the priest. The problem with this is that the sons of Eli are wicked men and have polluted the sacrifices of God. God comes to Eli and warns him of the impending judgment upon his family if he does not straighten things out. God reminds Eli, in this verse, that He had promised that Eli's house would be able to hold the office of the priest as long as they served God, but because of their disobedience, God is now only promising that they can hold this office as long as they honor Him. God said that those who would honor Him, He would honor. Those that despised God and His commandments, God would lightly esteem. What God was trying to get across to Eli was that past blessings don't guarantee present blessings if we do wrong. He wanted Eli to realize that if God was going to continue to bless his family then his family would have to do right.

Well the same is true for us today. We cannot rely on the past blessings that God has given to our nation. If our nation is going to continue to have the blessings of God upon her, then she is going to have to do right. If we as Christians are going to be blessed of God, then we cannot rely on the past blessings of God upon us or our family. If we are going to continue to keep the blessings of God upon us, we must live right today.

As I travel around the country, I run into people daily with the mentality that God will continue to bless us because of what we have done in the past. We must remember, God does not look at the past to determine the blessings of today.

29

God looks at what we are doing right now to determine whether or not He will bless us right now.

Let me ask you this question, if God looked at your work for Him in the past month and determined the amount of blessings that He was going to give you, how many blessings would you receive? We must constantly live our Christian lives trying to win the blessings of God upon our lives. We must live in such a way that every action we do is to try and get God's attention so He may bless us. Are you living so God can bless you or are you relying upon the past for God's blessings? Only what you do today will determine how much God will bless you.

When Doing Good Doesn't Pay

Judges 20:26
"Then all the children of Israel, and all the people, went up, and came unto the house of God, and wept, and sat there before the LORD, and fasted that day until even, and offered burnt offerings and peace offerings before the LORD."

Has it ever seemed in life that doing good doesn't pay? Have you ever come to the point in your life when it seemed as though every time you did good bad came out of your good? There is a reason why God allows this to happen.

In this story, the children of Israel were trying to do right. The tribe of Benjamin refused to correct a problem that happened in one of its cities, so the rest of the tribes of Israel went to God and asked counsel of God whether they should go up against Benjamin and destroy the men of this city. God told them to go up against this city, and when they did, several thousand of their men died. The men of Israel did not despair and asked God again if they should go up against this city; God told them to go up. Again, the battle turned against them, and they lost several men. It seemed as if every time they obeyed God something bad happened. Finally, we see God came through for these people, and they won the battle.

I give credit to the children of Israel because they did not give up on doing right and listened to God even when everything didn't seem to turn out right. Let me give you several quick thoughts that will help you when good does not seem to pay back good dividends.

First, God is always right! When good doesn't seem to pay, you must realize that God is always right. We don't always know why God doesn't allow good to immediately pay, but we must always realize that God is always right.

Second, God may be testing you to see if you truly trust Him. Many times God doesn't allow good to immediately pay

31

just to see if we truly trust Him. God's silence in our life is a test to see if we will continue to do right whether or not right seems to pay. We must be careful that we don't do right just because it pays well, we must do right because right is the right thing to do. God not coming through immediately may be a test that He is putting us through to see if we truly do trust Him.

Thirdly, if we will continue to do right, good will pay good dividends. Let me remind you that Romans 8:28 is still in the Bible and that it still says *"...all things work together for good to them that love God."* *"All things"* means even what you are going through. Let me also remind you that Galatians 6:7 still says, *"...for whatsoever a man soweth, that shall he also reap."* Good will eventually pay back good dividends if you will just keep doing right.

I do not know what you are facing today. I know at times it seems that doing good may only bring bad, but let me remind you that God's Word is always right and has **NEVER** been wrong. Let me encourage you that whatever good you are doing, God notices it and you will eventually reap what you have sown if you will just keep doing right. Whatever you do, DON'T GIVE UP!

Be On Time

1 Samuel 13:11-12
"And Samuel said, What hast thou done? And Saul said, Because I saw that the people were scattered from me, and that thou camest not within the days appointed, and that the Philistines gathered themselves together at Michmash; Therefore said I, The Philistines will come down now upon me to Gilgal, and I have not made supplication unto the LORD: I forced myself therefore, and offered a burnt offering."

When I read this story, I believe many times we blame the wrong man for what has happened in this story. Saul, I believe is not wholly to blame for his wrong doing. Now don't misunderstand me, I don't believe in passing the buck to someone else and blaming our shortcomings on others. I am a big believer in taking personal responsibility for our own actions. One thing is missed in this story and that is that Samuel did not come at his appointed time. Samuel apparently had promised Saul that he was going to come at a certain time, and Samuel did not keep his own appointment. Because of Samuel not being on time, Saul offered a burnt offering which he had no business doing. Though Saul was ultimately to blame for his own wrong, I believe that the tardiness of Samuel led to this wrong. If Samuel would have been on time, maybe he could have salvaged Saul from doing wrong. We will never know. We do know one thing; Samuel's tardiness certainly hurt many others.

Those who know me best know one thing that I am a stickler for and that is being on time. I do not believe there is a good excuse for being late. Being tardy is nothing more than a lack of character and a sin against God. We must understand, if we say we are going to be somewhere at a certain time, then we have given our word. For us to not be on time is nothing more than lying. We never know what our tardiness will cause others to do. We never know if our being late will cause others to do wrong. I would hate to think that my being late caused someone to go into sin. I know you may

33

think this is being petty, but God has always been on time and I believe we should be on time as well.

Being on time takes planning. You must figure out what time you are supposed to be at a place. Then, you must figure out how long it takes you to drive there. Then, you must figure the time it takes you to get ready to go. Once you have all of this figured out, then you can subtract that time from the time you are supposed to arrive and that is when you must start getting ready. Being late is simply poor planning. You can be on time if you choose to be on time.

Whatever you do, be on time for everything that you are going to do. Be on time for church. Be on time for work. Be on time for school. Be on time for soul winning. Be on time for a lunch engagement. Just be on time. Don't fall trap to the flaw in life of constantly being late. Be a person who is known for being on time. Don't ever let it be said of you as it was of Samuel; that because of your tardiness you caused another to do wrong. Just be on time all the time, and you will never have to worry about this being said about you.

Jealousy Kills Teamwork

1 Samuel 18:8
"And Saul was very wroth, and the saying displeased him; and he said, They have ascribed unto David ten thousands, and to me they have ascribed but thousands: and what can he have more but the kingdom?"

Nothing will destroy teamwork more than jealousy. Inside this verse is the story of David and Saul after the slaughter of Goliath. What a great victory God had given to Israel through the hand of David. With Israel working together they were able to do great things. Now as they come home from the battle, the ladies of the city were singing the song, *"...Saul hath slain his thousands, and David his ten thousands."* I can only imagine King Saul as he heared the first part of the song, how his heart must have been lifted up in pride as he thought the ladies of the city were welcoming him back. Then came the remainder of the verse where they ascribed to David ten thousands. When Saul heard David getting more praise than he, we immediately see the ugly eye of jealousy creeping into the heart of Saul. What a tragedy that Saul let this little song destroy his spirit toward a very loyal servant. What a tragedy that Saul was willing to let jealousy kill what teamwork had done for Israel.

Yet, the same thing happens on the job, in the church and in our society all the time. If we are not careful, we can get more wrapped up in the accolades of people than realizing how much teamwork can accomplish.

When trying to accomplish something, we cannot get jealous of someone because they get more praise than us. We must realize that we are all on the same team and though one may get more praise than the other, without the team the victory would not have been won. It takes teamwork for great victories to be won. It takes teamwork for the giants of life to be defeated. It takes teamwork for great causes to flourish. Superstars do not win championships. Teamwork wins championships, but jealousy can destroy a championship team.

In our churches, we must be careful not to let the praise of others cause us to become jealous. If we let jealousy creep into our churches, then our churches will cease to accomplish great things. Pastors cannot become jealous of another pastor who gets recognition because his church is bigger. That will kill us! We all need to work together to accomplish great things for God. When someone receives praise, we should be excited that God has blessed someone in that matter. When we get past the stage of worrying about who will get the recognition for the work being done, then great things can happen. I love the quote that says, "It is amazing how much you can accomplish when it doesn't matter who gets the credit." When everyone is concerned with just doing the work of God and not about who is going to get the credit for doing the work, then it is amazing the unity and the work that will be accomplished.

Let us be careful not to let our jealousy over someone else's recognition destroy the teamwork that we have going for us. Let us remember, in God's work there is no place for jealousy, there is only place for teamwork. When jealousy starts creeping in, great works cease because jealousy kills teamwork. Teamwork in the work of the Lord will accomplish great things.

Better Things To Come

Hebrews 11:13-15
"These all died in faith, not having received the promises, but having seen them afar off, and were persuaded of them, and embraced them, and confessed that they were strangers and pilgrims on the earth. For they that say such things declare plainly that they seek a country. And truly, if they had been mindful of that country from whence they came out, they might have had opportunity to have returned."

One of the most important things that we can learn in life is the principle of burning our bridges. We notice that in this passage of Scripture that all the saints of God looked for a better city. We notice that it says they embraced being a pilgrim and confessed that not only were they pilgrims in the land they dwelt in, but also strangers. In other words, they did not get too comfortable in the land in which they dwelt. Instead, they lived in that land looking for a better city, but then comes the key to them continuing on in this manner. The Bible states in this verse that they stopped being mindful of the country from which they came, and instead, accepted the seeking of the city in which God wanted them to dwell.

Herein is one of the keys of the Christian life. First of all, we must firmly settle in our hearts that we are not of this world. We must stop embracing this world, and start embracing the world to which we are going. We must stop getting so comfortable in this world that we stop looking for the city of promise. Too many Christians are setting up stakes in this old world. No wonder they have not the faith to step out and do great things for God. If you are ever going to do something great for God, you must not get too comfortable in this world. In other words, stop living for the possessions of this world.

Then secondly, we will never be successful in the Christian life until we burn the bridges to the past. Notice, if they had been mindful of the country from whence they came, the Bible says they would have gone back. Sometime in your life you must burn your bridges to the past. Accept and embrace the present. Until you embrace the present, you will never do great things for God. Too many people leave something in the past and always hold on to the hope of just maybe going back someday. This will never work in the Christian life. You must decide to completely burn your bridges and settle in your heart that you will never go back. Embrace the stage of life you are in or the place of life in which you dwell. Until bridges of the past are burnt, you will never completely be able to do for God what He wants you to do.

The success of your Christian life is dependent on these two things: not getting too comfortable in this present world and embracing where you are by burning the bridges to the past. Do you have bridges that need to be burnt? Is there still something you hold onto from the past? Decide now that you will never go back to the past, and embrace where you are in the present. Set up stakes in the present, seeking a better country. If you will stop living in the past and getting comfortable in this world, then that better country is waiting for you.

Don't Dig A Pit For Yourself

Proverbs 26:27
"Whoso diggeth a pit shall fall therein: and he that rolleth a stone, it will return upon him."

In the Bible, we find that God classifies sin in different ways. For instance, God calls some sin iniquity, some transgressions and some sin He calls evil. The worst of all sin is evil. Now I know that all sin is wrong and all sin is bad, but evil is especially wrong because of the degree to which it affects others. Evil is doing wrong with the intent to hurt someone. Evil is not just sinning, but it is committing sin with the purpose of trying to hurt someone.

God warns us in this verse to be careful about digging a pit for someone else to fall into because very likely we will be the one who falls into the pit. He again intensifies the warning by telling us not to try and roll a stone upon someone to hurt them because the stone will end up coming right back on us. What God was trying to get across to us is, when we make plans to try to hurt someone or to destroy someone it will end up backfiring on us, and we will be the one who is destroyed.

I think of several stories like this in the Bible. I think first of the story of Haman and Mordecai. Haman had such a hatred for the Jews that he had moved the king to have all Jews destroyed. Yet there was only one Jew that he despised and even hated. This Jew was Mordecai. His reasoning for hating Mordecai was because Mordecai would not bow down to Haman as Haman would pass by. This ate Haman up to the point that he started building gallows to have Mordecai hung on. To keep this story short, the very gallows that were built to kill Mordecai ended up being the gallows that Haman was hung on. Why? Because when you dig a pit to destroy someone else you will end up falling into that very pit.

I also think of the story of Joseph's brothers who had literally dug a pit and thrown Joseph in it. Their intent was to sell him into slavery and let the hand of his master kill him. This plot turned on them as years later their lives were at the mercy of the hand of Joseph. Joseph could have had them killed but did not because he was a better man than they. Again, they dug a pit to hurt someone else, and the pit ended up being the hurt of those who dug it.

All I am trying to say is, never become a person who sets out to destroy someone else. This is a very evil sin. It matters not what a person has done to you, never be guilty of living to see someone destroyed. We must realize that God writes everything down, and God will reward them for their deeds and what they have done to you. Though we may not like God's timetable of justice, God's justice is much better than what we could ever do to a person. You see if you try to destroy someone, then you have become no better than them. We must live with ourselves, and we must be able to sleep at night. We will have a hard time doing this if all we do is live to destroy someone else.

Just remember that life is too short to live with this type of attitude. Decide to let whatever has happened to you go, and move on realizing that in God's timing He will take care of them. If you don't, you will one day find yourself in the very pit of life that you wanted them to be in. That pit is misery. Trying to make someone else miserable will only make you miserable. Don't be guilty of digging a pit for someone else.

"Thank You" Is Not Hard To Say

Esther 2:21-23
"In those days, while Mordecai sat in the king's gate, two of the king's chamberlains, Bigthan and Teresh, of those which kept the door, were wroth, and sought to lay hand on the king Ahasuerus. And the thing was known to Mordecai, who told it unto Esther the queen; and Esther certified the king thereof in Mordecai's name. And when inquisition was made of the matter, it was found out; therefore they were both hanged on a tree: and it was written in the book of the chronicles before the king."

Packed inside the story of Esther the queen is a principle that reminds us not to forget some of the small things of life.

Esther had not been queen for a long time when this story happened. Mordecai found his place at the king's gate every day, and Mordecai pretty much knew all that was going on in the kingdom. As Mordecai sat at the gate, he heard two of the king's chamberlains plotting to kill the king. Their hatred for the king was so great that they decided to risk their lives to have the king killed. Somehow Mordecai overheard the plans of these men and Mordecai, being a good man, felt it was important to let the king know of this plot. So Mordecai contacted Esther and told her about the plot. She quickly told the king of the intention of these men, and after an investigation into the matter and finding out that the rumor was true, these men were killed.

Now you would think that the king would be very grateful to Mordecai for what he had just done for him. Just think, if it were not for Mordecai, this king probably would have died. Instead, because Mordecai notified the king, he was now alive. Yet after all of this, the king never one time sent a note of thanks or even left his throne to go and say "thank you" to Mordecai. How ungrateful and inconsiderate of the king.

41

If the truth be known, there are many people today just like this king who go through life and never say "thank you" to those who have done something nice for them. What an ungrateful society we live in today. It is almost a society that believes everybody owes us. I believe everybody ought to make a habit in their lives to say "thank you" to those who have done anything at all for us. Writing a short note of thanks is not real hard and does not take a lot of time, especially considering when someone has done something for you.

Don't you be guilty of being a person who is ungrateful. Instead, be sure people know when they do something for you, that you will show your appreciation to them. I have learned in life, if people know that you will show appreciation for the things they do for you, you will find that they will be more likely to do nice things for you again. Not that we should be grateful because we will get more things, but we should be grateful because it is the right thing to do. Learn to say "thank you" anytime someone does something for you. A simple "thank you" will go a long way to those looking out to make sure you are taken care of. If you live not expecting people to do things for you, then being grateful will just be common place for you.

In-Law Problems Are Easy To Solve

1 Samuel 19:10-12

"And Saul sought to smite David even to the wall with the javelin; but he slipped away out of Saul's presence, and he smote the javelin into the wall: and David fled, and escaped that night. Saul also sent messengers unto David's house, to watch him, and to slay him in the morning: and Michal David's wife told him, saying, If thou save not thy life to night, to morrow thou shalt be slain. So Michal let David down through a window: and he went, and fled, and escaped."

There is a reason why there are so many in-law jokes around. The reason is that most people don't know how to handle their in-laws in the right manner. The truth is most in-law problems happen because the mate whose parents are causing the problems has not put their foot down themselves.

Saul was jealous of David to the point that all Saul wanted to do was have David killed. Now we know the story well and that this all goes back to the slaying of Goliath. Saul thinks that David is out to get his throne, which was the furthest from David's thoughts. Yet Saul tries to kill David, and he escapes out of the way of the javelin that Saul had thrown. David went home to his wife Michal, who was the daughter of King Saul, and told her what had happened. During this time it was found out that Saul was sending messengers to the house of David to have him killed. Michal, loving her husband and wanting to keep him alive, tells him to escape and that she would handle her dad. As you read the story, later on you find that she had deceived her dad so that her husband could escape. In all reality what Michal was doing was choosing David, her husband, over her dad, King Saul. This choice was a dangerous choice as Saul could have had her killed for treason. She knew the severity of this decision, but she loved her husband and chose her husband over her own dad.

If every married person would learn from this story, it would solve just about every problem you have with your in-laws. I truly believe that most in-law problems could be solved if the child of the in-laws would step up to their parents and tell them that they are going to choose their mate, if they must, over them. When you get married you chose to leave your parents and be married to your spouse. That means, if the day ever comes when you have to choose between your parents and your spouse, the right thing to do is always choose your spouse. That was the promise you made the day you got married.

In-laws can be a blessing as long as each side knows their obligations and their boundaries. Don't let in-laws be the destruction of your marriage, but instead set your boundaries and you will find that your in-laws can be your friends and helpful to your marriage.

The Eyes Of The Lord Are Upon You

1 Peter 3:10-12
"For he that will love life, and see good days, let him refrain his tongue from evil, and his lips that they speak no guile: Let him eschew evil, and do good; let him seek peace, and ensue it. For the eyes of the Lord are over the righteous, and his ears are open unto their prayers: but the face of the Lord is against them that do evil."

We are warned in this Scripture to avoid evil and to do good. The reasoning behind this is that God's eyes are watching the righteous and how they live.

This thought gives me encouragement and yet it is sobering to think that God is watching me. Dear saint of God, let me remind you that God sees you. He sees you when you are doing good, and He sees you when you are doing bad. He sees you when you are present in the good places, as well as He sees you when you walk into the place of sin. This very thought should motivate you to live a clean life knowing that the eyes of the Lord are upon your every step and every action.

Yet, let me go a different direction as I believe this verse takes us. Not only are the eyes of the Lord upon us to watch how we live, but His eyes are also upon us to watch for our prayers and to watch over us to protect us. This means at this very moment God sees what you are doing. I am reminded of what a great preacher said to me as I was eager to do more for God. He simply told me to wait on God because He knows my name and address and knows how to get in touch with me when He is ready to do so. Let me remind you God knows your name, address and where you are. Because of this, He knows and sees what you are doing. He sees the good that you are doing though no one else sees it. He is watching you as you do good and are wondering if anyone sees the good that you do.

45

But one other source of encouragement from this verse is that God's ears are open to our prayers. That word *"open"* means He is waiting to hear your prayers right now. His ears are always waiting to hear the prayers of His people. So you wonder, does God even know who you are? Well not only does He know who you are, He also knows where you are and is waiting to hear from you at every moment. What encouragement this should bring to every saint of God.

So today, as you go through your normal routines of life, keep in mind that His eyes are upon you watching everything that you do. But also, keep in mind that He is waiting to hear your voice through prayer. Call upon Him for His ears are open to your prayers.

Temptation To Crown

James 1:12
"Blessed is the man that endureth temptation: for when he is tried, he shall receive the crown of life, which the Lord hath promised to them that love him."

In this chapter of the book of James we are told that temptations will come. Now the temptations that God is talking about are not a temptation of sin. Verse 13 says that God will not tempt any man with evil. The temptation that God is talking about in this verse is the temptation of trials. Trials do come in life, but as God talks about trials He shows us the stages through which we will go if we will endure trials.

First, we see in verse 2 that the trial will come. He says that we will fall into divers temptations. In other words, it won't just be one trial but a variety of trials that will come our way.

Second, we learn that trials will try our faith. Yes, one of the purposes of trials is to test the strength of our faith. Not only will a trial cause us to be uncomfortable, but it will also try or test our faith.

Third, we see in verse 4 that trials test our patience. So one of the benefits of trials is that our faith is tested, but so is our patience. This means that our patience and faith will grow through the trial if we let the trial have its perfect work in our life.

Fourth, after our faith is tried and our patience is tested, we must come to the point in our life when we will decide to endure our trial. We must decide that we are not going to quit when the trials come. We must understand that sometimes trials are not going to leave us, so we must settle in our hearts that we are going to endure this trial no matter how long it is going to take.

Fifth, we see that because we endure the trial, blessings will come. If we hang on long enough and do not quit, we will eventually find that because of trials, blessings will begin to roll into our lives. Blessings only come, though, if we endure the trials.

Last, we see reward will come. Notice in this verse that those who endure the trial will receive a crown of life. I believe eventually the trials that we face in life, if we endure them, will become a crown for us. If we will only keep going, they may become the thing that causes us to be used in a great way.

So decide right now that no matter what trial comes your way, you will endure it long enough so the blessings of life will come. Decide right now that you will use that trial as a crown in your life to help others.

Are You Loving God?

1 John 4:20-21
"If a man say, I love God, and hateth his brother, he is a liar: for he that loveth not his brother whom he hath seen, how can he love God whom he hath not seen? And this commandment have we from him, That he who loveth God love his brother also."

Many people have asked me over and over again, "How can I love God?" This verse tells us one of the ways that we can love God. I can love God by loving the brethren. Notice this verse says that if I don't love my brother then I do not love God. So, that would mean that if I wanted to show God that I love Him then I need to make sure that I love the brethren. I want you to notice, it did not say to love the brethren who are easy to love. It just says the brethren. It does not say to love those who can love me. It just says to love the brethren. In other words, when I love a brother who is unlovable, I am loving God. When I love a brother who is hard to get along with, I am loving God. When I love the bus kid who comes to church and may be a little rowdy, I am loving God. When I love the nursing home patient who is my brother, I am loving God. I believe we have this thought messed up in our churches today.

But then as we look at verse 21, God takes this thought one step further by not only telling us how we can love Him, but now He is making this a commandment from Him to love our brethren. God wants us to understand, this is no longer a choice; this is a commandment of God. God commands us to love the brethren. So, whether they are lovable or unlovable, we are commanded to love the brethren, and by loving the brethren we are showing our love to God.

My question to you is this, how much do you love God? Do you find yourself only showing love to those who are lovable, or are you the type of person who loves everyone in the church? Let us go about this week showing God how much we love Him by following His commandment to love the brethren.

Unto The Angel

Revelation 2:1
"Unto the angel of the church of Ephesus write; These things saith he that holdeth the seven stars in his right hand, who walketh in the midst of the seven golden candlesticks;"

Seven times in chapters 2 and 3 we see God speak to the churches. Each time God spoke to the church He chose to speak to the church through the man of God. We notice the phrase, *"Unto the angel of the church..."* The word *"angel"* means "messenger." The messenger of the church is the pastor of the church. There are several things we can take from this.

First, when God wants the church to do something, He will tell the pastor. Many church problems could be solved if every church and Christian in that church would accept this truth. Most church problems are caused by people who try to challenge the authority of the pastor.

Second, it is important that the pastor is listening for the Word of God. Every pastor needs to take their responsibility very seriously. Now I believe most pastors do, but the pastor of the church must be careful that he does not let anything sidetrack his attention from hearing God speak to the church. Not only must he listen for when God speaks to him, but he must also tell the church what God says whether it is popular or not.

Third, the church should listen to the man of God when he speaks. It does not matter that God speaks to the pastor if the church is not listening to the pastor. When the pastor speaks to us, we must be listening. Not only should we be listening, but we must also realize that the pastor is saying to us what God has told him to say. This means we should not get upset when he says something that we do not like. There are times when what God tells the man of God to speak to the church is not always going to be popular. Let us as a church unit, from the pastor to the church member, fulfill our position by listening for God to tell us what to do, and by doing what God tells us to do through the man of God.

A Sharp Sword

Revelation 2:12
"And to the angel of the church in Pergamos write; These things saith he which hath the sharp sword with two edges;"

We know from Hebrews 4:12 that the Word of God is likened unto a two-edged sword. Hebrews 4:12 says that God is the One Who holds that Sword. John 1:14 tells us Jesus is the Word of God which means He is the Sword. Now notice that the sword is a sharp sword. This would mean that the sharp sword will pierce that at which it is swung.

What is happening in our day is, we keep on trying to dull the sharp sword so that it does not hurt as much. We have tried to take the sharpness away by changing the Word of God. Leave It alone. In Its condition It can pierce down to the inner parts of the heart where sin is harbored. This is one of the reasons why we believe the King James Bible 1611 is the Word of God for the English speaking people. If It is not the Word of God then we have lost the sharpness that can pierce to the *"dividing asunder of soul and spirit."*

We have tried to change It by taking away the inspiration of the Word of God. You see, if the Word of God that we hold is not inspired, then the sharpness of that sword has been taken away. This is one of the reasons why the King James Bible 1611 must not only be preserved, but It also must be inspired because if anything is taken away from the original condition then It has lost its sharpness.

One of the other ways we have tried to change It is by taking away the sharpness of our preaching. Too many people have tried to take away the sharp preaching so it does not offend people. Now we should never do this. The intent of the Word of God being preached in Its purity is to pierce through the hard hearts of men. When the heart is pierced it will hurt, and some will get mad. But this is the purpose of the sword being sharp. This is why a person should not get mad at the preacher when he preaches the Word of God. If he preaches the Word of God like he should, it will hurt at times.

Let's be careful about trying to take away the sharpness of the Word of God. Let's be careful about trying to take the sharp sword away and replacing It with a dull sword. There is a reason why God wants It sharp, now let us not be a people who try to change the reason why God made His Word sharp.

The Mystery Of God

Revelation 10:7
"But in the days of the voice of the seventh angel, when he shall begin to sound, the mystery of God should be finished, as he hath declared to his servants the prophets."

Do you enjoy a good mystery book? Isn't it enjoyable when you are able to watch a good mystery that ends well? According to the Bible, God has chosen to keep Himself as a mystery to us. He has chosen to keep parts of Himself and the Bible as a mystery to us.

When the angel of God came down with a book in his hand, we learned that there will be seven thunders that begin to utter some things. As John heard the voices of the thunders speak, the Bible states that he was about to write what they were saying but was told not to write them, but to seal the sayings. Then this verse states that these thunders would sound the mystery of God.

What an interesting statement that is said about God. The word *"mystery"* means "something wholly unknown or kept cautiously concealed." In other words, God is telling us that there will be some things in the Bible that will be kept a mystery to us. He is also saying that there are some things about God Himself that will be kept a mystery to us.

There is no person alive who will ever know everything about the Bible or about God. God chooses to keep some things in the Bible shut up to our understanding. He chooses to keep some things about Himself a mystery to us so that we cannot understand everything. This is why there are some things in the Bible that just don't make sense to us because God has kept them as a mystery. Sometimes in the Bible it may seem that the Bible contradicts Itself. We must always understand the Bible NEVER contradicts Itself, It has just been kept as a mystery to us until God chooses to open our understanding to understand the mystery.

Because of this, the Bible will never become old to the one who chooses to study Its pages. The Bible will always reveal Itself anew to the one who studies It. Each time you read It God will open another mystery up to your understanding. Likewise the same can be said about God. Everyday we can learn something new about God if we will just spend time with Him.

Christian, don't let the mysteries of the Bible and of God confuse you or discourage you. By faith, trust God that one day He will reveal what you need to know about that mystery. When we are ready, He will open our understanding and then that which is a mystery will be open to our eyes.

Their Works Do Follow Them

Revelation 14:13
"And I heard a voice from heaven saying unto me, Write, Blessed are the dead which die in the Lord from henceforth: Yea, saith the Spirit, that they may rest from their labours; and their works do follow them."

What a powerful statement that God makes about these saints of God who have died. He says that after their death *"their works do follow them."* This is a wonderful statement that any Christian should desire to be said about them when they die. Several things come to my mind as I think about this little phrase.

First, you must have some works in order for these works to follow you. The truth is most Christians in our churches today would have no works that would follow them. When the Bible talks about their works following them, It is talking about ministries. These Christians had ministries in which they worked that were still going on even after they were gone. If your works are going to follow you, then you must get involved in the ministry to have your works and ministries continue after you are dead. These ministries cannot go forward unless you as a Christian will get involved in the ministry for Christ.

Second, what kind of works will follow you once you are dead? This is a very worthy question that every Christian should answer. I am afraid that some Christians will not like the works that follow them for their works are of the flesh and not the works of God. Every Christian needs to ask themselves if they died, would they want the works they are presently doing to follow them?

Third, how many works do you have that will follow you? Some will have the wrong works following them. Others will not have any works following them. This is what I am talking about. Notice the word *"works"* in this verse is plural meaning there was more than one work. Christian, will you have more than one work following you once you are gone? Have you helped more than one Christian, or led more than one person to Christ, or worked in more than one ministry? Will you have more than one work to follow you?

Lastly, don't let the saints that are gone on to Heaven down. Those of us still living need to carry on what the saints before us have done, and make sure we don't change the doctrine or the philosophy for which these previous saints stood. Let us be sure to let their works follow them.

Small And Great

Revelation 20:11-12
"And I saw a great white throne, and him that sat on it, from whose face the earth and the heaven fled away; and there was found no place for them. And I saw the dead, small and great, stand before God; and the books were opened: and another book was opened, which is the book of life: and the dead were judged out of those things which were written in the books, according to their works."

In the day of the Great White Throne Judgment, prestige is not going to matter. Notice the *"small and great"* stood before God. It did not say only those who no one knew. It did not say only the down and out of society. No, it said that the small, as well as the great, will stand before God.

One day those who are great in our society will stand before God. Whether they believe it or not, this will not change the truth that they will stand before God. In that day, they will have no excuse. In that day, their argument will not stand. In that day, they will stand before a holy God and nothing they use as an excuse will stand. God will not be impressed with their persona or the money they have made in this life. God will not be impressed with the titles they carried here on this earth. God will only accept one thing; is their name written in the Lamb's Book of Life? This is the only thing that truly matters.

To those who are great in this society, if you do anything in life, you had better settle your eternity. This can only be settled by accepting Jesus Christ as your Saviour.

To those who are religious leaders, especially religions that do not follow Christ, you had better settle the fact that Jesus is the only way to Heaven, and accept Him. To those in life who are oppressed by the "great" people of our society and yet you are saved, do not despair, their day is coming.

Though they may oppress you in this day, there is coming a day when they must stand before God.

Are you ready to meet the Lord today? Is your name written in the Book of Life? I didn't ask if you are great in society, I simply asked if you are ready? This question must be answered now while alive on this earth or else you will answer this question some day at the Great White Throne Judgment.

Feelings Don't Always Give Feelings

Ephesians 4:17-19
"This I say therefore, and testify in the Lord, that ye henceforth walk not as other Gentiles walk, in the vanity of their mind, Having the understanding darkened, being alienated from the life of God through the ignorance that is in them, because of the blindness of their heart: Who being past feeling have given themselves over unto lasciviousness, to work all uncleanness with greediness."

This may seem like an odd title, but I believe you will understand what I am talking about once I am done.

God tells of the Gentile people and how they walked or lived their lives. God said that these Gentile people, in the region of Ephesus, were a people who lived according to the vanity of their mind. He goes further to explain this statement by saying that they eventually were *"past feeling."* In other words, God was saying these people were a people who lived by their feelings. This is why God talked about them living in the vanity of the mind. When you live in the vanity of the mind, you will live by feelings.

The problem with this type of living is found in the last verse where God says that they were *"past feeling."* God was showing us that when you live by feelings eventually those feelings will no longer give you the satisfaction that they used to. So, because the feelings no longer give you the feeling you want, you will go elsewhere to get that same feeling. In the case of these people, they went to a lascivious lifestyle. This is a lifestyle that fulfills the lust of the flesh; no matter what it may be.

This is the danger of living by feelings. When those feelings no longer give you what you want, you will look elsewhere to get those same feelings. The problem with this is, again you will find yourself not being satisfied because feelings will never satisfy.

God's people need to be careful of living by feelings. I am not against having feelings, and I believe that Christians need to get some feeling back into their Christianity. But, you must not let feelings dictate how you are going to live. You must not let feelings dictate what you are going to do today. There will be days when you are tired and feelings will not be present. If you live by feelings, on those days, you will find yourself not doing what you are supposed to do. But if you live by principle and by schedule, even on the days when you don't feel like doing right, you will do right because principle and schedule tell you to do right.

Be careful not to get caught up in the "feel good" Christianity. If you live by feelings, then one day you will find yourself doing things you never imagined because feelings will eventually lead you down a path that cannot satisfy. Instead, get caught up in doing right because principle tells you to do right.

The Test Of Great Leadership

Genesis 2:19
"And out of the ground the LORD God formed every beast of the field, and every fowl of the air; and brought them unto Adam to see what he would call them: and whatsoever Adam called every living creature, that was the name thereof."

After everything in the earth had been created, God told Adam that one of his jobs was to name every beast of the field and fowl of the air. It is interesting to me that God brought these animals and birds to Adam to see what he would name them. Notice that whatever name Adam gave to these creatures, God left that as the name.

I believe a very important lesson on leadership is found in this verse. No doubt God knew what He wanted to call the animals that He had created. Certainly if God had the power to create these creatures, He also had the wisdom and knowledge to name them. Instead of doing this work Himself, He delegated the task to Adam. Here comes the lesson, once God delegated the task to Adam, He let whatever Adam named the animals be their names. Maybe, I do not know, God thought some animal should have been called something different, but because He delegated this task to Adam, God was secure enough in Himself to let the names of these animals be what Adam called them. This is one of the signs and characteristics of great leadership.

Every leader must learn that once you have delegated a task to a person, you must let what they do go forward without you interfering as long as it will not hurt the cause of what you are trying to do. Though you as a leader may be able to do the task better than the one to whom you delegated the task, you must let them do what you asked the follower to do. First of all as a leader, if you interfere in what you ask the follower to do, it will cause insecurity in them. Not only will you cause insecurity, but you will cause friction in your relationship with them because they will not know how to please you. Great leadership is not intimidated by someone else doing something a little different than how you would do it. As a leader, if you had the confidence in this person to hire them or to choose them to help you, then you must have the confidence to let them do their task. Don't undercut them in the task because doing this will eventually cause problems in your relationship.

God let Adam do what He had asked him to do even if God thought something should be done differently. Likewise leaders must let their followers do the delegated task even if the leader thinks they can do the task better. In so doing, you will create a bond of trust between follower and leader that will eventually cause your leadership to flourish.

Making A Difference

Jude 1:21-22
"Keep yourselves in the love of God, looking for the mercy of our Lord Jesus Christ unto eternal life. And of some have compassion, making a difference:"

The greatest need in the Christian life is people who are difference makers. Difference makers are a people who are not satisfied with just accomplishing something, but while accomplishing something they make a difference in the lives of others. Churches are in need of pastors who are difference makers. Sunday school classes are in need of teachers who are difference makers. Schools are in need of teachers who are difference makers. Society in general is in a great need of Christians who will be difference makers.

We find in the above verses the key to being a difference maker. First of all, in order to be a difference maker we need people who will keep themselves in the love of God. Now notice the Bible did not say to keep themselves in love, but in the love of God. You see, the love of God is much greater than the love of man. The love of God will cause us to love the unlovely. The love of God causes us to love those who cannot give love back. The love of God loves someone because they need to be loved. The love of God looks beyond the condition of the person and sees them as an individual who is simply in need of some love from someone. God says that nobody will ever become a difference maker without keeping themselves in the love of God. This means this is a purposeful act. If we are going to stay in the love of God, this is something we must work at. When God says to keep yourselves, He insinuates that we must guard ourselves from letting other things pull us away from living in His love. We can never and will never make a difference in the life of people without first having God's love flowing through us. It is His love and His love only that can make a difference.

Secondly, though God says that not only must we keep ourselves in the love of God, but we must also have compassion for people in order to make a difference in their lives. Compassion is more than just feeling sorry for someone and their condition. Compassion is sorrowing with someone in their hard times and in their heartaches. It is literally suffering with someone as they go through hard times in life.

You give me a preacher who suffers with someone in their hard times and I will show you a preacher who will make a difference in the life of that individual. You show me a Sunday school teacher, youth worker, bus worker or a teacher in a Christian school who suffers with a person as they go through a hard time and I will show you someone who will make a difference in that person's life.

We must be very careful that we do not become so busy with our schedule that we forget why we are in this business. If we cannot help people when they are at the bottom of life and suffer with them when they are there, then we will never make a difference in people's lives.

Now let me ask you a question, are you a difference maker? Do you make a difference in the lives of people for good when you cross their paths? God wants His people to be difference makers. The only way you will be a difference maker is to keep yourself in the love of God and have compassion for people; suffering with them when they suffer. This is what makes difference makers.

Obedience Finds Grace

Genesis 6:22
"Thus did Noah; according to all that God commanded him, so did he."

This chapter starts out by saying in Genesis 6:8, that *"Noah found grace in the eyes of the LORD."* Then we come to this verse which I believe shows us why Noah found grace in God's eyes. Though in this day the whole world was wicked and though the whole world's imagination was evil continually, there was one man who decided that he was not going to live like this. Instead we see Noah obeying everything that God had commanded him to do. This is why he found grace in God's eyes. This is why God salvaged Noah from the coming destruction upon the earth.

You see, it matters not what the whole world is doing, ultimately it is our choice to do right. If the whole world's imagination is evil, we can still have a clean and wholesome mind because it is a choice. This is the only hope for a nation. This is the only hope for a world. The hope is that there will be at least one person who can find grace in God's eyes by obeying every commandment of God.

What we must ask ourselves is this, if God were to look at the whole world today, would He find us obeying all His commandments and thus finding grace in His eyes? Or would God find us living like everyone else? Let us keep our eyes off of what the world is doing and let us keep our eyes upon what God wants us to do.

Yes, we must live in the world, but the world does not have to live in us. Let us strive daily to keep the world from living in us by obeying all of God's commandments. In doing so, we will find that we too can find grace in the eyes of God.

The Average Or The Exception

Job 1:8-11
"And the LORD said unto Satan, Hast thou considered my servant Job, that there is none like him in the earth, a perfect and an upright man, one that feareth God, and escheweth evil? Then Satan answered the LORD, and said, Doth Job fear God for nought? Hast not thou made an hedge about him, and about his house, and about all that he hath on every side? thou hast blessed the work of his hands, and his substance is increased in the land. But put forth thine hand now, and touch all that he hath, and he will curse thee to thy face."

Here we have the story of God and Satan conversing with each other about God's servant Job. God asked Satan if he had considered His servant Job. Satan's answer is interesting. He said he had but that the reason why Job was such a good person was because God had blessed him. Satan told God that if he would begin to touch Job with trials and heartache that Job would curse God to His face.

Now where did Satan get this idea about Job? Let me tell you. We find previously in this chapter that when Satan originally appeared before God that God asked Satan where he came from. Satan's response was that he had been going to and fro throughout the whole earth. You see, Satan was telling God that as he had walked up and down throughout the earth he had seen others who, when blessed by God, would say that God was good. But he had also seen the same people and when hard times would come they turned on God and cursed God. Satan thought that Job would do the same as the average man alive and would curse God when hard times came. The great thing about Job was that he was not like the average person. Though others, when hard times came would curse God, Job would not lose his integrity. In fact the Bible says that in all that Job went through he did not sin with his lips. Job was not just average; Job was the exception to the average.

I wonder if God were to ask Satan today if he had considered His servant ____ and God would say your name. What would Satan's response be about you? Better yet, what would your response be about you? Are you the type of person who praises God when you're on top of the mountain, and then when you are in the valley you complain about God? Or are you the type of person who is the exception to everyone else? No matter whether you are on the mountaintop or in the valley, God is still good to you? What are you, the average or the exception? Let me tell you, what this world needs are some Christians who will be the exception and not the average. This world needs to see Christians who will prove Satan wrong when he judges us. The sad part is that Satan has just about pegged most Christians.

Let us determine in life not to be average. Let us determine in life to be the exception and show a world that we will serve God and praise God in the valley just like we do on the mountaintop.

Make Me A Blessing

Genesis 12:1-3
"Now the LORD had said unto Abram, Get thee out of thy country, and from thy kindred, and from thy father's house, unto a land that I will shew thee: And I will make of thee a great nation, and I will bless thee, and make thy name great; and thou shalt be a blessing: And I will bless them that bless thee, and curse him that curseth thee: and in thee shall all families of the earth be blessed."

The greatest difference between Christians who God uses and those whom He does not use is what they do with the blessings that God has given to them. There is probably no Christian alive who does not want to be blessed of God, but the reason why they want to be blessed determines whether God will bless them greatly or not.

We notice in this passage of Scripture that God promised Abram that once he left the country in which he was raised God would bless him in a great way. God told Abram that if he would have faith and trust God to leave his homeland that great blessing would follow. In fact, God promised the blessing that would follow was that in Abram all nations and families will be blessed; if only he would obey God.

We notice though that in order for Abram to be blessed he had to first of all have faith in God. You will never experience the great blessings of God in your life without having faith in God. Faith in God is the foundation of great blessings. It is only through faith that we can please God, so then it would only be through faith that great blessings from God can come.

Then we notice that in order for blessings to come obedience must follow our faith. God told Abram that he must leave his homeland. The blessings of God on Abram's life were totally dependent upon his obedience. Likewise, if we are going to experience the blessings of God on our life then we must let obedience follow our faith. You see faith in God and obedience go hand in hand. It is truly hard to have faith in God if you do not obey, for obedience in God is an act of faith.

But now we come to what I truly want you to see and that is why God chooses to bless us. Notice in verse 2 that the reason why God blessed Abram was so that he would be a blessing to others. The verse says, *"... and I will bless thee, and make thy name great; and thou shalt be a blessing..."* Do you see what God is saying? God said that He would bless Abram so he would be a blessing to others. This is the true reason why God blesses us. God blesses us so that we can be a blessing to others. God does not bless us so that we alone can enjoy the blessings. God wants the blessings that He sends our way to be shared with others.

Christian, when is the last time you allowed others to be a partaker of the blessings of God in your life? When is the last time you took the blessings that God has given you and went out to help someone else and were a blessing to others?

I love the song, "Make Me a Blessing." This truly is what every Christian should desire. Today as you go out among those whom God leads along your path, be a blessing to them. Make it your prayer to God to make you a blessing to someone today. Be sure to realize that when God blesses you that the purpose of that blessing is to make you a blessing to someone else. You will find that the more you use your blessings to bless others the more God will choose to bless you.

Separation, A Command For Everyone

Genesis 17:24-27
"And Abraham was ninety years old and nine, when he was circumcised in the flesh of his foreskin. And Ishmael his son was thirteen years old, when he was circumcised in the flesh of his foreskin. In the selfsame day was Abraham circumcised, and Ishmael his son. And all the men of his house, born in the house, and bought with money of the stranger, were circumcised with him."

Circumcision in the Bible is a type of separation. God wanted His people to be different from the rest of the world so He commanded the Israelite men to be circumcised.

The interesting thing about this passage of Scripture is that Abraham was ninety years old and Ishmael was thirteen years old. Why is this? Because separation is for every age! Separation is for the son as well as the dad. Separation is for the old and the young alike. Separation does not have an age factor; separation is a command that every age is to follow.

We then notice that the Bible states that all the men of Abraham's house were to be circumcised. Now what was the purpose of this? The purpose is that separation is for every position. Separation is not just for the leadership of the church; separation is also for the lay person. Separation is for the pastor and the church member alike. Separation is for the staff member as well as for the church member. God does not want only those who have position in His church to be separated from the world, He wants everyone to be separated from the world. You see, separation is not commanded because you hold a position in the church; it is expected of every saved person because separation is for the saved and not just for those who hold position.

As I travel as an evangelist in this country to different churches, I see over and over again that many churches don't get understand separation is for everyone. Far too many times I see churches where the pastor expects his staff to live separated lives but he will not preach it from the pulpit. This is wrong! Likewise I see parents who live a separated life and hold the standards that God expects His people to have, and then I see their children who look like the world. This ought not to be!

The whole reason why God wants His people to live a separated life is because God wants His people to be different from the world. God wants the world to be able to look at His people and know that they live differently.

So let me ask you this question, can the world see a difference in your life? Could a person look at you and tell that you are a Christian because of the life you live? If not, then you have some changing to do. Let us be careful not to make separation only an issue for those who hold positions in the church, but let us make separation an issue for Christians; an issue that Christians are to be different from the world.

God's Blessings Are For You Too

Genesis 19:29
"And it came to pass, when God destroyed the cities of the plain, that God remembered Abraham, and sent Lot out of the midst of the overthrow, when he overthrew the cities in the which Lot dwelt."

All throughout history there have been great men of God who have built great works. I can think of men of recent years such as J. Frank Norris, Lee Roberson, Lester Roloff, Charles Spurgeon and Jack Hyles. This list could go on and on. I personally had the privilege of being under the ministry of Dr. Jack Hyles for thirteen years of my life. The one thing I noticed about being under his ministry is that many times people were living off of the blessings of Dr. Hyles instead of getting the blessings of God upon their own lives. What I mean is many times people were being blessed by God in their ministry all because of Bro. Hyles. Then when they would leave, they thought this blessing would follow them and many times they would fall flat on their face. All of this happened because they failed to get God's blessings upon their own life.

Lot seemed to always be in debt to Abraham. It was Abraham who raised Lot after his parents apparently died. It was Abraham who saved Lot from captivity from the people of Elam. Again, we see Abraham saving Lot from being destroyed by God with the people of Sodom and Gomorrah. It seems that the constant theme of Lot's life is for Abraham to save him from the trouble in his life. Lot was living off of the blessings of Abraham instead of getting the blessings of God upon his life. Somewhere Lot needed to realize that God's blessings were for him as well as Abraham. But until Lot started living a life where God could bless him, he would never realize the blessings of God upon his life.

We should never be satisfied with being blessed because of God's blessing upon someone else's life. We should not try to live off of the blessings of some man of God or some great person. We should get the blessings of God upon our own lives so we can experience God's blessings first hand.

Are you living off someone else's blessings? Let me remind you that God's blessings are not prejudice. God's blessings are for you just as much as they are for great men of God. If you are willing to live the life which they live and walk with God like they walk with God, then you too can have the blessings of God upon your life. Never be satisfied with just eating the crumbs off of the table of someone else. Get the blessings first hand from God. God wants to bless you! If you will do what it takes to get these blessings, then God will bless you.

At The Set Time

Genesis 21:1-2
"And the LORD visited Sarah as he had said, and the LORD did unto Sarah as he had spoken. For Sarah conceived, and bare Abraham a son in his old age, at the set time of which God had spoken to him."

God is always on schedule. We notice that the Bible states that Sarah conceived at the set time. No, it was not the timing of Abraham and Sarah, but it was the timing of God. Abraham and Sarah thought they should have had a child many years prior. Abraham and Sarah thought God just wasn't going to come through for them in this area of their life, but God is always on time and will come through at the set time.

We must realize that God's timing is never the same as man's timing. God does not work off of man's calendar or schedule. Though we may live in a day when we expect everything to happen right now, God does not work that way and God knows what is the best timing for our lives. We must realize, God can and will come through as He has promised.

What is it today that you are wondering if God is ever going to come through for you on? Have you been praying for something for several years and it seems as if God is never going to answer that prayer? Let me just remind you that whatever the issue is in your life that you need God to come through, at the set time He will come through. It may seem that if God doesn't come through right now that you are facing complete destruction, but rest assured that God knows your situation. God knows what the best timing is and because of this, at the set time, He will come through.

Now don't be impatient with God and try to work things out as Abraham and Sarah did. When you do this you will always hurt yourself as well as others. Abraham and Sarah, because of their impatience, have caused heartache for many generations that followed them and continue to this day. When we become impatient with God and try to work things out ourselves, we always cause hurt to ourselves and even to many whom we influence. Learn to wait on God realizing that at the set time He will come through.

God Led Me In The Right Way

Genesis 24:48
"And I bowed down my head, and worshipped the LORD, and blessed the LORD God of my master Abraham, which had led me in the right way to take my master's brother's daughter unto his son."

One of the hardest things a person can do in life is to discern what the right way is and what the wrong way is. My thought is the majority of people in life want to walk the right way. I seriously doubt that most people want to make the wrong decisions in life and end up walking down the wrong way. Most people want to be led in the right ways.

As the servant of Abraham tells the story of how Abraham had sent him on a quest to find a bride for Abraham's son Isaac, he explains how quickly God answered his prayer in finding Rebekah. The servant makes a great statement as he explains what he did after he found her so quickly. He says he *"blessed the LORD God"*, and here comes the statement I want you to notice, *"...which led me in the right way..."* He said that God was the One Who led him the right way in this journey.

This is always the case when a person will trust God. God says in Proverbs 3:5-6, *"Trust in the LORD with all thine heart; and lean not unto thine own understanding. In all thy ways acknowledge him, and he shall direct thy paths."* He is saying that if we will just trust Him with all our heart He will direct our paths, and we notice in this verse that this path is the right way.

Somewhere in our lives we must learn to start trusting that God wants the best for His people. We must understand that in life there is always a right way and a wrong way. There is never a gray area that is neither right nor wrong. It is always right or wrong, and this is why we must trust God to lead us down the right way of life.

Someone may say, so how do we know this right way? The right way is always the Bible way. The Bible is God's Word to us. This is why we must study the Bible everyday and follow what the Bible tells us to do in everything, even when we don't understand why God tells us to do something a certain way. The Bible will always lead us to the right way. God promises us that His Word will lead us down the right paths of life. So, why not trust the God Who has never failed us?

Are you searching for the right way in your business? Then why not pray to God and ask Him to lead you down the right path in your business, and then go and obey His Word. He will lead you to the right way. In what area of life are you searching for the right way? Is it in the finding of a mate to marry? Is it in finding which career path to follow? Is it in where to live? Is it in rearing your children? Is it in handling your finances? Is it in choosing which church to go to? Whatever the area is in which you are searching for the right way, God is the One Who knows the right way for you. Ask Him to lead you in that right way, study His Word to find what It says to do, obey whatever He tells you to do in the Bible, and you can rest assured that He will lead you down the right way.

Use Your Common Sense

Genesis 27:18-20
"And he came unto his father, and said, My father: and he said, Here am I; who art thou, my son? And Jacob said unto his father, I am Esau thy firstborn; I have done according as thou badest me: arise, I pray thee, sit and eat of my venison, that thy soul may bless me. And Isaac said unto his son, How is it that thou hast found it so quickly, my son? And he said, Because the LORD thy God brought it to me."

One of the greatest needs in our society today is the need for people to use their common sense. As I travel around the country, I am amazed at how little common sense most people have. Even when it comes to listening to the news and listening to those who are in leadership of this country, a lack of common sense seems to be very evident.

In the story of Jacob and Esau, Isaac, their father, had asked Esau to go and make him some venison meat so that he could have a meal together with him and impart upon him the family blessing. As you study this passage of Scripture, we see Rebekah, the mother, stepping in and telling Jacob to make some venison meat and bring it to his dad so he can be blessed instead of Esau. Rebekah and Jacob contrived a plan to deceive Isaac because he was almost blind. As Jacob came in with the venison meat, Isaac was amazed that the meat was prepared so quickly knowing that it would take some time to find a deer, kill and dress it and then cook it. Isaac knew something was up, so he asked whom he thought was Esau, to come close to him so he could smell and feel him. Isaac knew Esau was hairy and Jacob was not. Without going into the rest of the story, what amazes me about this story is that Isaac used every sense that God had given him but the most important one, common sense. You see, common sense would have told him that it was impossible to find and prepare the venison that quickly. Yet instead of using the most important sense, common sense, he went ahead and trusted all his other senses.

Common sense is a wonderful thing that God has given to everyone. Because God has given us common sense, He expects us to use it. It is amazing that Isaac used every sense that God had given him but the most important one: common sense.

Most of the Christian life can be determined through common sense. The truth is, God's commands are common sense living. Most of the decisions that all of us need to make in life can be settled through common sense living. The next time you must make a decision in life, why not ask what common sense says to do. You will find most of the time this will help you in making decisions.

Unresolved Issues

Genesis 32:6-7
"And the messengers returned to Jacob, saying, We came to thy brother Esau, and also he cometh to meet thee, and four hundred men with him. Then Jacob was greatly afraid and distressed: and he divided the people that was with him, and the flocks, and herds, and the camels, into two bands;"

Unresolved issues from the past have a way of eating at us until we take care of our part of the issue. After all these years, twenty-one years, Jacob was still afraid of Esau, though Esau had moved on with life. We see in this story that Jacob was getting ready to move back to his homeland when he realized that he needed to get things right with Esau. So in order to do this, he sent messengers ahead to try and soften the blow with Esau thinking that Esau still wanted to kill him because of how he stole the blessing of his father. As the messengers came back, they told Jacob that Esau was coming to meet him with a host of men. Immediately Jacob thought the worst. The reason he thought the worst is because he had an unresolved issue with Esau that he had never taken care of. All these years it had eaten at him and worried him, yet to no avail. The unresolved issue had resolved itself without him doing anything.

We must make sure that our issues from the past get resolved so they do not eat us up. Instead of worrying about the past, why not face the past and take your lumps so you can move on with life. We should realize that most of the unresolved issues from the past do have a way of resolving themselves. Now this does not mean that we should not make right something that we have made wrong. What this means is most of what we worry about is useless. If we are going to clean our conscience, then we need to make sure that we clear up what we have done wrong so we do not have to carry unresolved issues around with us for the rest of our life.

Another thing we should realize about unresolved issues is that it hurts us more than it hurts the person with whom we have this unresolved issue. Notice, it had probably eaten at Jacob a whole lot longer than it did Esau. Can you imagine the years of inner turmoil that Jacob had to live with? This is why you must settle your unresolved issues with people early on. If you don't settle these problems, they will only get worse inside of you instead of better.

Lastly, we must give our unresolved issues to God for Him to work out instead of us trying to work them out by ourselves. When you look at this story, you can see that God had already worked out this issue in the heart of Esau. This was much better than Jacob trying to do this. Everything that Jacob tried to work out ended up coming back to bite him. If you have an unresolved issue with someone, then my advice is to commit it to God asking Him to work in the heart of the one which you have wronged, and ask God to soften their heart. When God does the work in the heart and prepares the way for you to right the wrong, then you will find it much easier to solve the issue with the other person. If you try to resolve things yourself, you will most likely make it worse. Ask God to help you in solving the issue with them, and you will see that God's way of solving these unresolved issues is much better than our way.

Stop carrying around unresolved issues and face them. You will have to face them some day, so the best day to face them is today so that you can live your life without unresolved issues eating away at you.

Pull Your Own Weeds First

Genesis 38:24-25
"And it came to pass about three months after, that it was told Judah, saying, Tamar thy daughter in law hath played the harlot; and also, behold, she is with child by whoredom. And Judah said, Bring her forth, and let her be burnt. When she was brought forth, she sent to her father in law, saying, By the man, whose these are, am I with child: and she said, Discern, I pray thee, whose are these, the signet, and bracelets, and staff."

This story reminds me of a situation I had to deal with years ago. The situation was with a person who had some severe family problems who was trying to tell another family that they needed to get their family problems in order. I remember how I was somewhat amused that here was a person who had their own problems trying to tell another person that they need to get their problems taken care of. I was asked to help with this situation and so I gladly did. My counsel was mainly given to the person trying to tell the other family to deal with their family problems. I told them that they had better pull the weeds in their own garden before they start going around telling others to pull the weeds out of their garden.

This illustration reminds me of what happened here in these verses. As we read the whole story, Judah unknowingly hires his daughter-in-law, whom he thinks is a prostitute, to have some pleasure with her. Three months after this situation he finds out that his daughter-in-law is pregnant out of whoredom. Judah angrily responds to bring her forth to have her killed. As the men came to take her, she told them that she is pregnant by the man who owns the bracelet and signet that she gave to them. Of course, these things belonged to Judah. How amazingly his tune began to change when he found out that he was the one that got her pregnant. Here is a man who was trying to have his daughter-in-law killed for the same sin that he had committed. He was just like most people today who are more interested in telling others to pull their weeds when they have weeds in their own garden.

How careful we must be about trying to tell others to take care of the sin in their lives. I would advise everyone, before you start going around and thinking you are the spiritual police and telling others to clean up their lives, you ought to go look at your own garden, and pull the weeds out of your own garden first. Too many people have weeds growing in their own garden and then want to tell others to pull their weeds first. Especially to preachers I say, yes you must always preach truth, but be sure you are pulling weeds out of your garden before you start demanding that others pull the weeds in their garden. I think if most people will look at the weeds in their own garden they will realize that they have plenty of weeds to pull before they start telling others to pull weeds.

Let us be a people who inspect our gardens first. Let us be a people who work on pulling our own weeds first before we start pointing out the weeds in others' gardens. I would imagine that we can help others more when there are no weeds in our gardens.

Opportunity Seekers

Genesis 39:7
"And it came to pass after these things, that his master's wife cast her eyes upon Joseph; and she said, Lie with me."

One of the greatest destroyers of successful men is that of having an affair with some woman who is truly only after him because of his position. Over and over you hear the stories of men who have fallen prey to this trap. Now I am not looking down on these men or thinking that I am better than them, for I know anyone is capable of doing this. I am simply making an observation about a fact.

Joseph is now a servant to a very wealthy man by the name of Potiphar. As was Joseph's character, he gave his best to his master and because of this, Joseph began to move up in position. Finally, one day Potiphar noticed how hard Joseph worked and how much he could be trusted and promoted him in his household to head slave. The Bible states that he made him overseer over his house and put all that he had under the hand of Joseph. What power Joseph had obtained. Yet once this happened, we see the wife of Potiphar propositioned him to have an affair with her, to which Joseph rightfully rejected.

Maybe one of the most overlooked parts of this story is the phrase in this verse, *"And it came to pass after these things..."* It was only after success started coming towards Joseph that the wife of Potiphar cast her eyes upon him. She was not so much attracted to him as she was his success. She had become an opportunity seeker who was after his success more than she was after him. She could see, as her husband could, how Joseph was moving up and she wanted to be part of this success. So, the only way she knew how to be a part was to have an affair with him. If he was not careful, Joseph could have ruined his life. Joseph, if he listened to her flattery and to the opportunity, could have ruined everything that God had planned for him.

Every man needs to take warning from this story. When success comes a man's way there will be opportunity seekers who will come after you. Watch out! These whores are not so much after you as much as they are after your success. You ought not be flattered that once success comes you start being noticed. Where were these women when you were at the bottom of the rung? Every man must realize right is right all of the time, and no position offers you the right to do wrong. Joseph acknowledged this, and God blessed him in an even greater way because of his stance for right. Just be alert when success starts coming your way, for these opportunity seekers will start knocking at your door. Men, when they come, watch out and slam the door! Nothing will ruin you quicker than for you to open the door and enjoy something that will only last for a season. These opportunity seekers will leave you once success leaves you, for they are not after you, they are after what your success will give to them.

Don't become prey to this tactic. Always keep a watchful eye out for these types of women. Especially to married men I say, remember to whom you are married. Remember she loved you before success came your way, and if she has stuck with you up to this point, she most likely will stick with you when tough times come again. Just a friendly warning to watch out for opportunity seekers!

Discreet And Wise

Genesis 41:33
"Now therefore let Pharaoh look out a man discreet and wise, and set him over the land of Egypt."

When leaders go about to set someone into a position, they must be careful about whom they choose. When a business owner is deciding whom he should hire for a position, he also should be very careful whom he hires.

As always, God gives us the answers on how to hire for a position or how to decide whom we should place in a position of leadership. Joseph told Pharaoh that when he decided to place someone in this position to help him run the land of Egypt during the time of famine, he should look for a man who was discreet and wise. These two words will help any person in hiring and placing someone into a position.

The word *"discreet"* means "to be cautious in making decisions." In other words, when hiring someone you must hire someone who is not rash in making decisions. A person of leadership or a person who holds a position that is responsible for making decisions must be very cautious that they make the right decisions every time. They cannot be a person who jumps to conclusions. A person who is quick in making decisions will hurt you in the long run.

But we also notice that a person who is hired for an important position should not only be discreet and cautious in making decisions, but the Bible says they should be wise as well. The word *"wise"* in this verse is talking about knowing how to implement the discreet decision that has been made. When you place someone in a position of leadership, you not only want this person to be cautious in the decisions that they make, but you also need someone who knows how to implement these decisions in the best manner. If you, as the owner of a business or a leader of leaders, must always tell someone how to implement the decisions made, then you do not need that person. People of authority must learn to make cautious decisions and must also learn how to implement those decisions in the best way possible. When you find a person like this, you have found a person who is worthy of a leadership position.

Two lessons that will help us concerning what we have learned. First, when followers must choose someone to lead them, then followers need to find someone who is discreet and wise. Especially if you are choosing the pastor of a church, you must choose a man who is discreet and wise. Whoever leads you will ultimately decide what your future will be, and you do not want someone to lead you who is quick to make decisions or who does not know how to implement ideas and decisions.

Secondly, everyone should strive to be discreet and wise in their lives. One day everyone will become a leader in some area of their life. Most will eventually become a parent, which is a leader. So now is the best time to start practicing being discreet and wise in your decisions. If you become discreet in your decision making now and learn to be wise in implementing these decisions, then you will find that this process will become so much a part of you that it will become second nature when implementing decisions.

A Capable God

Genesis 47:5-6
"And Pharaoh spake unto Joseph, saying, Thy father and thy brethren are come unto thee: The land of Egypt is before thee; in the best of the land make thy father and brethren to dwell; in the land of Goshen let them dwell: and if thou knowest any men of activity among them, then make them rulers over my cattle."

During the time when the events of this verse occurred, the world was experiencing a time of famine. You may recall that before this event occured, Jacob had been sending his sons to Egypt to buy food because there was no food in their own land. The world economy was bad, rain was non-existent and people had to sell everything they had just to be able to have food to eat. I would imagine that this was very similar to the Great Depression days in the United States.

Yet, it is interesting that even in a time of famine, God is capable of taking care of His people. We must always remember that God is never worried about the world's economy when it comes to taking care of His children. Philippians 4:19 says, *"But my God shall supply all your need according to his riches in glory by Christ Jesus."* This verse did not say He would supply your need only in time of plenty, it says He will supply all your need. God's promises in the Bible are not dependent upon how the world's economy is running. God's promises in the Bible are sure no matter how the world is doing financially.

You will notice that Pharaoh told Joseph to give his father and brothers the best of the land. God not only has the power to take care of us in lean times, but God also has the power to give us the best of the land during lean times. We must realize that God is very capable of taking care of His people in the lean times just as He is capable of taking care of them during plenteous times. The good part is, He not only gives us just what we need, but God can give us the best of the land. When praying for God to supply your need, don't pray for God to give you a second rate answer. Pray to God realizing that He is capable of giving you the best. Why would God give us the best during the hard times? This proves to the world that even when times are tough, God is strong enough and powerful enough to take care of His own. When God gives His children the best of the land, then He proves His power to a lost world and He receives the glory not us.

Though we may live in an economy that is struggling, God is certainly capable of supplying our need if we will only trust Him. Stop doubting the power of God, and realize that God can supply your need in the tough times as well as in times of plenty.

All That He Had

Genesis 46:1
"And Israel took his journey with all that he had, and came to Beersheba, and offered sacrifices unto the God of his father Isaac."

When I was a boy, I was the type of person who always gave everything that I had no matter what I did. My mother drilled inside of me that I should do my best no matter what I was doing. So, because of this, I gave everything I had to whatever I was doing. When I played sports in high school, I gave everything I had during the practice time just like I did during the game. I just felt that if I gave everything in practice then when game time came I would not lack in skill or endurance because I was used to giving it everything and not leaving anything behind. This mentality has followed me to my adult years and even into the ministry. Those who have heard me preach would never doubt that I give all that I have when I am preaching.

One of the keys to being successful in life is giving everything you have to the task at hand. We notice in this verse that Israel took his journey, notice, *"...with all that he had."* This was not talking about all his possessions, for we read earlier in the book of Genesis that they were told to bring only themselves and their flocks and that they could live off of the good of the land of Egypt. This was talking about Israel giving all of his effort to go to the land of Egypt so that he could see his son before he died.

If a person is going to excel in life then they must make it routine to always do whatever they do with all that they have and leave nothing behind. You will never excel in the work force by giving a half effort at your job. Only those who give everything they have when they work tend to excel in the work place. It is interesting that the loafers on the job are not the ones who get promotions; it is those who work hard and give everything they have to their jobs who get promoted.

In our Christian life, if we are going to excel, we must give all of our effort in serving God. Maybe one of the biggest problems that we have in Christianity is half-hearted, don't care Christianity. I get fed up with this type of Christian. I am talking about the type of Christian who doesn't care that they give half of their effort towards serving God. Listen, if serving God is worth doing, and it is, then let's give all that we have towards serving God.

If our home life and our marriages are going to excel, then we must give all that we have to make these work. No home will excel with members of the family giving half-heartedly towards the family. No marriage will excel when you have husbands and wives giving half-hearted efforts towards making their marriage successful. The home and the marriage will only excel when those involved give all that they have to these areas.

What all of us need to do is live everyday, giving all that we have to whatever we are doing and leave nothing behind at the end of the day. So today, as you go through your day, give it all that you have in everything you do and see how the day ends up. If anything, you will feel better about yourself knowing that you have given your best.

Hang In There

Exodus 5:22-23
"And Moses returned unto the LORD, and said, Lord, wherefore hast thou so evil entreated this people? why is it that thou hast sent me? For since I came to Pharaoh to speak in thy name, he hath done evil to this people; neither hast thou delivered thy people at all."

There are times when the ways of God make no sense to us. We see in Exodus 4:31 that God had visited His people. After the people realized that God had visited them and that He was going to deliver them, their afflictions did not decrease but instead increased. Pharaoh was not as excited about the people being visited by God as they were. Because they came to him, Pharaoh increased their burden. What they thought should have been a decrease in their burdens ended up being an increase.

Now we don't always understand why God does things the way He chooses to do them. When God visits us, it does not always mean that life is going to get easier. In fact, the majority of the time when God visits us it will mean that life will get harder. We don't always see the whole picture and sometimes life must get harder in order for it to get easier. The Israelites did not see what God was going to do for them. God had to send those hard times in order for Pharaoh to let them go.

Now don't become discouraged when things start getting harder in your life. You just hang in there, and you will see God doing what He has promised He will do. You have prayed for God to visit you and maybe He has, but just because God has visited you and is going to do something great through you does not mean life as a whole will become a piece of cake. Most of the time after God visits us, life will become harder. This is to test us to see if we really want Him to do something great through us. What we must do when this happens is hang in there and wait for God's timing to come through. When it comes through we will see the mighty hand of God in a great way. So don't despair and keep going. God will come through for you like He said He will.

Are You Ready

Exodus 12:29-30
"And it came to pass, that at midnight the LORD smote all the firstborn in the land of Egypt, from the firstborn of Pharaoh that sat on his throne unto the firstborn of the captive that was in the dungeon; and all the firstborn of cattle. And Pharaoh rose up in the night, he, and all his servants, and all the Egyptians; and there was a great cry in Egypt; for there was not a house where there was not one dead."

Chapters 7 through 12 of Exodus are always very exciting chapters to read. Here you see the power of God revealed to Pharaoh and the people of Egypt. The final plague that God sent down upon these people, He called the plague of the Passover. The Passover was the final plague that God sent upon Egypt. He commanded His people to take a firstborn lamb of the flock and kill this lamb. They were to take the blood of that lamb and apply the blood upon the doorposts of their house. Whoever had the blood on the doorposts of their house would be passed over by the death angel that night. The angel finally came and we see that those who were ready did not see death in their family, but those who took it lightly and were not prepared saw the firstborn of their house die that night. What a terrible night this was. The text that we read says at midnight there was a great cry in the land of Egypt. They were weeping over the loss of loved ones who were not ready when the death angel passed over.

This story reminds me of another story that we read about in Matthew 25:6. It is the story of the ten virgins waiting for the bridegroom to come. It says in this verse, *"And at midnight there was a cry made, Behold, the bridegroom cometh; go ye out to meet him."* As these virgins went out to meet him, five of the virgins had no oil for their lamps and because of this, they were not taken in by the bridegroom. I wonder if some of the virgins in this story were crying because they missed their opportunity to meet the bridegroom.

Each of these stories remind me of the day when Christ is coming back to take His bride to Heaven. What a day this is going to be! There is only one way that we are going to be ready for this day. We must have the blood of the Lamb of God applied on the doorposts of our hearts. It is only the blood of Jesus that can save us and prepare us for the day when He comes to take His own to Heaven.

O, the urgency of the hour. We are close to that midnight cry. My question to you is, are you ready? Are you ready if He should come today? Are you ready, Christian, to meet the One Who has saved you from your sins? Lost person, has the blood of Christ been applied to your account or will you be left behind? How each of us should take inventory of our lives to be sure that we are ready. What heartache you will face if you are not ready. Yet, what joy will be yours if you are ready.

God, A Man Of War

Exodus 15:3
"The LORD is a man of war: the LORD is his name."

Though most people like to quote the verse, *"God is love"* this is only one side of the story of God. We look at this verse and see that the God of love is also a God of war. In the society that we live in today, we hear people say all the time that God is not for war. They like to quote that *"God is love"* and they are right when they say this, but this is only one part of a very great God. I want you to notice a few things about this verse.

Notice it says *"The LORD..."* This name LORD is Jehovah God; the self-existent God Who created this great world and is an all-powerful God. Yes, those who are saved serve a God Who is not made with hands as Buddha or Muhammad and other gods. We serve the all powerful, self-existent God Who has no beginning and will have no end.

Then the Bible says that God is a *"man of war."* I love it because not only is He the LORD, but He is a man. Not a man in the sense that He is a created being, but a man in the sense that He is manly. He is not a sissy God as this world paints Him. He is a manly God! A man in the sense of tough. A man in the sense that He is not a pushover. A man in the sense that He is not afraid to endure tough things. This verse says He *"is a man of war."* The completeness and greatness of God is seen in this statement. Not only is God a God of love, but He is also a man of war. Not only can He be tender and be our Comforter, but He is also a man of war. He can hold a child on His lap and say, *"Suffer the little children to come unto me..."* but He is also a man of war. Though this world, especially the liberals, do not like to admit this side of God, we cannot and should not deny nor ignore that God is a man of war. He is a God Who, that if need be, will fight wars for He is a man of war.

So let me say to the soldier fighting in a war, you are in good company! Even our God is a man of war. This means He knows the tough times you are going through, for He has fought wars Himself. He understands how others may portray you in a bad sense because He Himself has been portrayed in a bad sense. He knows the toughness of war because He has been there Himself for He is a man of war.

To those who are casual readers, let us not deny the fact that God is a man of war. Though liberals may try to say that God is not for war, we cannot deny this verse. If God is not for war, then how can He be a man of war? If God is a man of war, then that would mean He must believe in war for the right causes.

But let me also say, because He is a man of war, every Christian need not fear when they go through battles, for He being a man of war, is not afraid to stand with you through the battles. He will stand beside you for He promises in Hebrews 13:5, *"...I will never leave thee, nor forsake thee."* So whatever battle you face today, you can have confidence that God, as a man of war, is beside you in the battle and is fighting for you in the battle.

Murmuring

Exodus 16:8
"And Moses said, This shall be, when the LORD shall give you in the evening flesh to eat, and in the morning bread to the full; for that the LORD heareth your murmurings which ye murmur against him: and what are we? your murmurings are not against us, but against the LORD."

We find a very interesting statement in this verse when it says that the people did not murmur against Moses and Aaron, they murmured against God. Yet, when we read Exodus 16:2, it says that the people murmured against Moses and Aaron. Now why does there seem to be a discrepancy in these two statements? Simply put, when a person murmurs against authority they are murmuring against God. I am sure the people thought they were only murmuring against Moses and Aaron for not having a plan to feed them once they got into the wilderness. These people did not understand that Moses and Aaron were only obeying God when they lead them into the wilderness. When these people chose to murmur against Moses and Aaron about the food, in all reality, they were murmuring against God.

What is murmuring? Murmuring is complaining. Murmuring is more than just complaining, it is complaining in a mumbling low voice. Murmuring is like a person who, under their breath, complains hoping no one will hear them. This is what murmuring is. What the children of Israel did not understand is that God heard their murmuring and was not pleased with all their murmuring ways. There are few things we can learn about murmuring.

First, murmuring is like a disease, it will spread. I seriously doubt that all the people started murmuring at the same time about what they did not have. I think what happened was one person started murmuring, another heard it and it started spreading. How careful we must be that we don't become a source of the murmuring in our church, work place or home. Our murmuring will spread to others for it is like an infectious disease.

Secondly, God hears your murmuring. If only we would realize that someone does hear that complaining we do under our breath, and that person is God. If we realized that God hears what we are complaining and murmuring about, I would imagine that most people would stop their murmuring. Well let me just tell you, God does hear what you are murmuring about and He is not pleased when we murmur.

Thirdly, when you murmur against authority you murmur against God. Let me just say, you will find that murmuring is ALWAYS against authority. We murmur about how our boss is treating us or how our employer is paying us. We murmur about how the pastor is running the church. We murmur about how the school principal runs the school. We murmur about how our parents are rearing us. All this murmuring is against authority, but ultimately we are murmuring against God. We must realize that most of the time authority is only doing what God tells them to do and, when we murmur against them, we are murmuring against God.

Let us be careful about our murmuring. How sinful it is to murmur. When we murmur we are saying what God gave to us is not good enough. Don't be a murmurer! Be a person who is content with what you have. Realize that if we do murmur, God will hear it and God will not be pleased with what we are saying. Let us be a people who, instead of murmuring, count the blessings of God's goodness to us.

The Wickedness Of False Reports

Exodus 23:1
"Thou shalt not raise a false report: put not thine hand with the wicked to be an unrighteous witness."

It is important that before we say something about someone that we verify that it is true. God commands in this verse that we are not to raise a false report about anyone. In fact, God says that if we raise a false report about someone, we are no different than a wicked person who is a false witness in a trial case. A false witness in a trial case tries to put someone in jail because they hate them, and this is how bad God feels that it is for us to raise a false report against another person.

How careful we must be in saying things about other people. If we do not know something is true, it would be best that we never pass it along to anyone else. This is why we should never go off of hearsay about a person. When you go off of hearsay about a person, you have no idea whether the report is true or not. You are only going off of another person's word.

Before you say something about anyone, verify the information firsthand so that you will not be guilty of spreading a false report. I would rather never say anything about a person than to spread something and find out later that I was wrong. Like my mother used to say to me, "If you have nothing good to say about a person, then don't say anything at all." This would be a good rule of thumb to use when it comes to giving a report on a person.

If someone comes for advice about another person and if you don't know that person, then don't give any advice. Protect your name by only giving what you know as a true report because you have verified it personally. I guess we could use the rule of thumb that reporters are supposed to use when giving a report about someone; only give a report on someone when you can verify the information by two credible witnesses. Unless you have two credible witnesses I would advise you to keep your mouth shut. It can be mighty embarrassing to have to cover a report that was false. Not only is this embarrassing, it is wicked. Let's be careful about spreading false reports.

Keep Bothering God

Exodus 32:9-10
"And the LORD said unto Moses, I have seen this people, and, behold, it is a stiffnecked people: Now therefore let me alone, that my wrath may wax hot against them, and that I may consume them: and I will make of thee a great nation."

Israel had just committed the great sin of setting up the golden calf in the wilderness. Moses had been up in Mount Sinai for forty days receiving the commandments of God. After giving the commandments to Moses, God commanded Moses to get back down to his people because they had fallen into idolatry.

We see an interesting phrase while God is talking to Moses about Israel, *"...let me alone, that my wrath may wax hot against them..."* God was telling Moses not to bother Him about the people because He was going to destroy Israel and make of Moses a great nation. It is almost as if God was trying to bait Moses into begging Him for His mercy so He would not have to destroy Israel. It is almost as if He was begging Moses to bother Him on behalf of the children of Israel.

I really believe that God did not want to destroy Israel. I believe what God was looking for was someone to intercede for this nation. God just wanted someone to beg Him for His mercy so He would not have to destroy the nation of Israel.

I wonder though, is there someone that is bothering God for your nation? Is there someone to stand every day for their nation at the throne of God asking God to be merciful to their nation for the sins they have committed? O, how every nation needs an intercessor to God! Every nation needs someone who bothers God daily to keep His blessings upon their nation.

If the blessings of God were dependent upon you praying for your nation, how many blessings would your nation receive because of your prayers? Have you spent any time with God today bothering Him for your nation? I plead with everyone reading this thought; don't ever stop bothering God for your nation. Your nation needs you to stay at the throne of God and bother God for His blessing. Don't ever leave God alone for your nation. Beg and plead for your nation so that just maybe, God will revive your nation in spite of her weaknesses.

Business Advice From God

Exodus 34:12-14
"Take heed to thyself, lest thou make a covenant with the inhabitants of the land whither thou goest, lest it be for a snare in the midst of thee: But ye shall destroy their altars, break their images, and cut down their groves: For thou shalt worship no other god: for the LORD, whose name is Jealous, is a jealous God:"

Over and over again I see people make a mistake that causes bitterness and hardships. This mistake is going into joint business ventures. First of all, most joint business ventures end with people being hurt. Yes, they can work, but the majority of the time people end up with hard feelings. Friendships of a lifetime have ended all because of joint business ventures.

A very solemn warning is given by God to His people about joining up with anybody *"of the land."* His reason for being so careful about joining up with the people *"of the land"* is if they were not careful, they would ensnare themselves in the idolatry and worship of these people. In these verses, we learn some prerequisites that God has for us in deciding whether or not we should join up with someone.

First of all, they should be saved. You should never go into any business venture with someone who is not saved. When a person is not saved and you go into business with them, you are guaranteeing problems because you both have different masters. A lost person is sure not to understand the reasons why a Christian does things the way they do.

Second, you should never join someone who is still running with the crowd that is worshipping the wrong way. When you go into business with someone who runs with the wrong crowd, they are sure to pull you into their way of worshipping God which is wrong. You should only go into business with people of like faith.

105

Third, never join up with someone who worships and serves God differently than you. This is where most people mess up. Just because they are saved and go to church does not mean that you should go into a joint venture with them. If they have different philosophies and methods of serving God than what you were taught, then you should not join up with them. Not only will it cause friction between the two, but eventually they will lure you over into their way of thinking. Rarely does the stronger one pull the weaker one up. Most often the weaker one pulls the stronger one down.

Let's be careful with whom we choose to join. Do your homework concerning them, and make sure that you both are going the same direction otherwise heartache is sure to come.

He Knows Your Name

Exodus 39:14
"And the stones were according to the names of the children of Israel, twelve, according to their names, like the engravings of a signet, every one with his name, according to the twelve tribes."

As God explained to Moses concerning the garments for Aaron the priest, He told Moses that one of the garments that was to be made was a breastplate. This breastplate carries with it several wonderful meanings.

One of these meanings concerns God's commandment that there be twelve stones upon the breastplate. Each stone represented one of the twelve tribes of Israel. Yet there is even something better explained in this verse. God not only wanted the stones which represented the twelve tribes upon this breastplate, but God also wanted each stone to have the name of the tribe represented engraved upon the corresponding stone. Let me explain how this can help us.

Jesus is our high priest. With Jesus being our high priest, each of these symbols represents what Jesus is to us or what we are to Jesus. God wanted us to know that our name is on His heart. Notice that the stones with the engraved names are on the breastplate which rests upon the heart of the priest. God wanted us to know that we are never forgotten by Him. He also wanted to enforce this thought by telling them not to just write the names of the tribes on those stones but to engrave the names upon those stones. Engraving can never be worn out or wiped off. God wanted us to know that not only are we on His heart, but we are indelibly engraved upon His heart.

What a thought! To think that right now we are on the heart of God is amazing. Not only are we on the heart of God, but He knows our name. In a world that seems to forget about us and sometimes will run over us, God never forgets about us and He ALWAYS knows our name. You wonder if God knows who you are? Let me encourage you, not only does He know where you are and who you are, He also knows your name.

I remember awhile back while I was preaching at a church, an elderly gentleman came to me and started talking to me. As we talked he asked me if I remembered who he was. I responded by telling him I not only remembered his face but I called his name to let him know that I knew his name. It thrilled this man that I would know his name. I have good news for you Christian, not only does God know your face, and not only are you on the heart of God, but God knows your name as well. Throughout this day you can take solace in the fact that God knows where you are, who you are and He even knows your name.

Knowledge Brings Responsibility

Leviticus 5:1
"And if a soul sin, and hear the voice of swearing, and is a witness, whether he hath seen or known of it; if he do not utter it, then he shall bear his iniquity."

Leviticus 5:3
"Or if he touch the uncleanness of man, whatsoever uncleanness it be that a man shall be defiled withal, and it be hid from him; when he knoweth of it, then he shall be guilty."

Knowledge always brings responsibility. God is teaching His people in these verses the importance of taking responsibility for the sins which they have committed.

Notice two phrases, one phrase in verse 1 and the other phrase in verse 3. In verse one we notice the phrase, *"...then he shall bear his iniquity."* Then in verse 3 we notice the other phrase, *"...when he knoweth of it, then he shall be guilty."* In both instances, the sin was already committed and the sin was wrong. Yet, it wasn't until the person realized that they had sinned that they became responsible to God for what they had done.

God is a merciful God. God will wink at our sin if He knows that we do not realize that it is sin. It is when we know that we have sinned and do nothing about it that God holds us accountable. No doubt we are all sinners, and we all sin every day. But it is not the unknown sins which I have committed that God holds me accountable for, it is the known sins that I have committed which God expects me to deal with. I am not saying that unknown sin which I have committed is okay; I am saying it is the known sins which I have committed that God wants me to take care of.

We must realize that knowledge always brings responsibility. When we have sinned and will not deal with it, then not only have we sinned but we also have added

109

rebellion to this sin. This is why it is so important to deal with sin immediately; as soon as we know we have done wrong. God never approves of sin, but when rebellion comes in, God must deal with our rebellion.

I ask you, what is the sin you have committed that you have not dealt with? God will hold you accountable for this sin. If we want to have a good relationship with God, then we must be sure that we immediately deal with the sin that we have committed. Anything less than immediate response is rebellion against God. Be careful not to become calloused towards your sin by saying, "Everybody has sinned." Deal with your sin at the moment that you have done wrong so that you can have a clear and right relationship with God.

Don't Jump To Conclusions

Leviticus 10:16-19
"And Moses diligently sought the goat of the sin offering, and, behold, it was burnt: and he was angry with Eleazar and Ithamar, the sons of Aaron which were left alive, saying, Wherefore have ye not eaten the sin offering in the holy place, seeing it is most holy, and God hath given it you to bear the iniquity of the congregation, to make atonement for them before the LORD? Behold, the blood of it was not brought in within the holy place: ye should indeed have eaten it in the holy place, as I commanded. And Aaron said unto Moses, Behold, this day have they offered their sin offering and their burnt offering before the LORD; and such things have befallen me: and if I had eaten the sin offering to day, should it have been accepted in the sight of the LORD?"

A very important truth is taught in this story as Moses noticed that Aaron had not eaten the burnt offering that he had offered that day. It says that Moses was angry and approached Aaron to ask him why he had not done what he was supposed to do. The mistake that Moses made was he jumped to a conclusion before he had heard the whole story. If Moses would have listened to the whole story before making his opinion, he would have saved himself some stress and also some tense communication between himself and Aaron.

Every person should learn to never jump to conclusions about any situation before hearing both sides of the story. When you jump to conclusions, you end up embarrassing yourself and will have to make apologies for what you have said and done. This is why it is wise to listen to both sides before you make a decision. Jumping to a conclusion over an assumption will only cause you to look bad, as it did Moses. Wise people and wise leaders learn to listen to the whole story before making conclusions.

Parents, before you jump to conclusions over something that your child has done, you would be wise to

111

listen to their side of the story. School teacher, be careful not to jump to a conclusion after hearing only one side of the story. You should listen to both sides of the story before making any conclusion about what has happened. Leaders, be careful about jumping to conclusions over a situation when you have only heard or seen one side of the story. You can save yourself a lot of heartache and embarrassment if you will wait to make your conclusion over the situation until you have heard both sides of the story. Likewise, don't jump to conclusions over a situation you have heard on the local or national news. This is only one side of the story. Before you go out and start making your opinions about a story, you would be wise to wait until you have all the facts.

Jumping to conclusions is a terrible thing to do because you hurt the one side that you have not heard. Not only do you hurt that one side, but you also hurt your character. Listen to both sides of the situation and then make your decision or opinion. Jumping to conclusions will only make you look dumb and will eventually hurt your credibility if it becomes your pattern. Let us learn to wait when forming opinions or conclusions over a situation.

Customs And Manners

Leviticus 18:1-4
"And the LORD spake unto Moses, saying, Speak unto the children of Israel, and say unto them, I am the LORD your God. After the doings of the land of Egypt, wherein ye dwelt, shall ye not do: and after the doings of the land of Canaan, whither I bring you, shall ye not do: neither shall ye walk in their ordinances. Ye shall do my judgments, and keep mine ordinances, to walk therein: I am the LORD your God."

In all the years that I have traveled as an evangelist, I have had the privilege to travel to several foreign countries and preach. It is always an honor, whether in a foreign country or in the United States, for a pastor to ask me to come and preach to his people. As I traveled to each of these countries I learned that every country has their own customs and manner of doing things. Even in the United States, each region has its own customs and manner of doing things. In order to win the people over to me, I have learned when I am in these countries, to practice the same customs and manners that they do. For instance, in the Philippines when you greet people, not only do you shake their hands, but many times they will raise their eyebrows also as a way of greeting. In the States you would never do this, but in the Philippines this is their custom of greeting. So when in the Philippines I practice this custom to let them know that I do not think I am better than they are.

God, in our text, told Moses when Israel dwells in the land of Canaan, He does not want them copying the *"ordinances"* of the people of Canaan or of Egypt. God said instead of copying them, He wanted them to follow His commandments and His judgments; which is the Word of God. The phrase, *"After the doings..."* and the phrase *"their ordinances"* is simply talking about the customs and manners of these nations. What God was teaching His people was that when customs and ordinances go against the Word of God, you forsake the customs and ordinances and follow the

113

commands of God. God's Word always trumps any custom or manner of doing things.

Now we must be careful not to use our customs and manner of doing things as a crutch to do wrong. For instance, one of the things that irritates me is when church services start late. Many times preachers give me the excuse they start late because it is customary for people in their region to be late, therefore their people don't arrive on time. Now when the custom causes you to have a lack of character, you always do what is right and do not follow that custom. This is what God was teaching us in these verses. God is not against people having their own customs as long as these customs and manner of doing things do not cause a person to do wrong.

I do not know what the custom is where you live, but if your customs go against God's Word, then you need to forsake the custom for what the Bible teaches. We must be very careful that we don't let the customs of the land or the manners of the people be our crutch for doing wrong. If the whole world does wrong, we must still do right. Right is always right to do even if people around us think that doing right is against our own custom. Loyalty to God and His Word should be our ultimate loyalty, not the customs and manners of the people or a nation. Let us adopt the customs and manners of God to show a world that His customs and His manner of doing things is where true happiness lies.

Reverence God's Name

Leviticus 24:16
"And he that blasphemeth the name of the LORD, he shall surely be put to death, and all the congregation shall certainly stone him: as well the stranger, as he that is born in the land, when he blasphemeth the name of the LORD, shall be put to death."

A solemn warning from God is given to His people in this verse. The warning is to those who blaspheme the name of God. He tells the children of Israel that if a person blasphemes God, they should be put to death. God takes this sin very seriously. To establish capital punishment for blaspheming God means God takes it very seriously when someone blasphemes His name.

Now if God takes this sin this serious, we had better find out what the word blaspheme means so that we are not guilty of committing this sin. The word *"blaspheme"* means, "to blame God or to speak irreverently of God." In other words, God said that those who blame Him for their problems of life are blaspheming His name. This could include speaking irreverently about God concerning your trials. God does not mind if you tell Him how you feel, but what God wants from us is to speak reverently to Him.

Be careful Christian when you pray to God in anguish of soul that you do not blame God or speak irreverently to God during these times. God takes this very seriously. God never minds when we pour our heart out to Him about problems in life. What He minds is when we come to Him in an irreverent way blaming Him for our problems. In other words, when you speak to God, even when you are pouring out your heart, always keep in mind to Whom you are speaking. Never give disrespect to God when you are speaking to Him.

Now let me take this a little further. Though today we do not take someone's life from them when they blaspheme God, I do believe God is teaching us another lesson. We should not spend time with those who blaspheme God. I believe we should treat that person as if they were dead. In other words, don't acknowledge them. If a person starts blaspheming God in your presence, you should stop them immediately and tell them you will not put up with them blaspheming God. We should not be passive about this! We should stop people who blaspheme God because God is worthy of being spoken of reverently by everyone.

Last of all, let us be careful how we speak about God. Let us be sure that in hard times we don't become angry with God and speak irreverently to Him or about Him. Let us remember that God does not owe us anything. If we will remember that God does not owe us anything, I believe this will keep us from blaspheming Him. Never be guilty as a Christian of blaspheming the name of God. Let us keep His name and speak His name in high regard.

Righting A Wrong

Numbers 5:6-7
"Speak unto the children of Israel, When a man or woman shall commit any sin that men commit, to do a trespass against the LORD, and that person be guilty; Then they shall confess their sin which they have done: and he shall recompense his trespass with the principal thereof, and add unto it the fifth part thereof, and give it unto him against whom he hath trespassed."

Righting a wrong that we have committed against another is never an easy thing to do, but it is important to do if we are going to be right with God and man. In these verses, God shows us how to right the wrongs of our lives. The word that is important for us to understand in this verse is the word *"trespass."* In the Bible, God classifies sin in different categories. For instance, some sin is just sin, but there are other sins that are more than just a sin, they are sins of another degree that don't only affect us. The trespass sin is one of those sins. When a person commits a trespass, they are infringing upon the rights of another. In this chapter, God gives us a classic example of a trespass by using someone who commits adultery. Adultery is a trespass sin, for when you commit adultery, you are infringing upon the rights of your mate and of the mate of another. So, a trespass is not only a sin against God, but it is also a sin against another. God shows us how to right a trespass that we have committed. Remember, any sin that takes from another something that belongs to them is a trespass. How do we right something when we have trespassed against another person?

First of all we must admit our guilt. Notice the verse says, *"...that person be guilty..."* You will never correct a wrong that you have done against another person without first admitting your guilt. It is not just that you have wronged that person, but notice, you have also wronged God. Anytime we commit a trespass, we have wronged God and the person we have committed the trespass against. Without first admitting guilt, you will never be able to get this sin right.

The second step of getting right over a trespass committed is to confess the sin. Now I believe we ought to confess this sin to two people. First of all we ought to confess this sin to God. We have wronged God first when we commit a trespass. Admit your guilt to God without giving any excuses. Then the second person to whom we should confess our sin is the person whose rights we have infringed upon. This is the hardest step. If we are going to get our conscience cleared, we must admit our guilt to this person. This is not only good for us, but it is also good for the person whom we have wronged, for they need to hear you admit your guilt so they can move on.

The last step of righting a wrong is to recompense, or pay back the wrong that we have committed. Now in many cases this is hard to determine, but somehow you must get this paid back to them. If anything, when you confess that you are guilty to the person you have trespassed against, ask them what you can do to settle this wrong with them. According to the Bible, if they refuse for you to pay them back, then you are to pay the wronged amount to the LORD. Today this would be putting that amount of money in the offering plate at your church.

Without following these steps, you will never have a clear conscience. If you want to right a trespass that you have committed, then these are the steps that God prescribes for you to right your wrong. When you have done these steps, you will find that you feel much better about yourself and you will never have to walk around with a guilty conscience hoping that you do not cross the path of the one whom you have wronged.

Wholly Given

Numbers 8:14-16
"Thus shalt thou separate the Levites from among the children of Israel: and the Levites shall be mine. And after that shall the Levites go in to do the service of the tabernacle of the congregation: and thou shalt cleanse them, and offer them for an offering. For they are wholly given unto me from among the children of Israel; instead of such as open every womb, even instead of the firstborn of all the children of Israel, have I taken them unto me."

The tribe of Levi had a special place in the heart of God because, of all the tribes of Israel, He had chosen them to be His. When it came down to God giving each tribe their inheritance, the only inheritance that the tribe of Levi got was that they became the inheritance of God. What a special place these people had in the heart of God. Imagine being the ones whom God chose to be His inheritance. This was nothing to be taken lightly. To be the inheritance of God is better than having gold, silver or lands.

The Levites job was to be workers in the temple. Their job was to be the ones who assisted the priests in the work of the temple. They would be much like those in our churches today who help the pastor build the church of God. If the Levites position existed today, they would be the bus workers, youth workers and those who help in the ministries of the church.

In these verses, God was teaching us some things about these people that we can apply to our lives. God wanted them to give themselves wholly to Him. God was teaching us that those who are going to be His ministers in the church need to give their entire life over to one thing; the service of God. God is not satisfied with part of our life; He wants us wholly or entirely without anything being held back. If God is ever going to use us to the extent that we want Him to use us, we must give ourselves wholly to Him.

119

We should ask ourselves this question, what is it that God does not have from us yet? Is there something that we are holding back from God, something that He does not have? If God does not have us wholly then God cannot use us wholly. To whatever portion we hold ourselves back from God is the same portion that God cannot use us. O, how I would hate to think that God wanted to use me more, but I held Him back from using me because I had not wholly given myself to Him. I would hate to think that God had greater things in store for me as a Christian but He could not give them to me because I had not wholly given myself to His work. Let us strive to give ourselves wholly to God. Let us search our hearts and be sure that there is nothing that we have withheld from God. Withholding things from God will keep us from being used in a greater way.

D.L. Moody, at a prayer meeting with his friend, Henry Varley, heard him say, "The world has yet to see what God can do with, and for, and through, and in a man who is fully and wholly consecrated to Him." D.L. Moody later decided to be that man, and my, how God used him in a mighty way. I say to you today, the world has yet to see what God can do with one man who is wholly committed to Him. Decide today to be that person who is wholly committed to Him and see what God can do through you.

Moving At God's Speed

Numbers 9:21-22
"And so it was, when the cloud abode from even unto the morning, and that the cloud was taken up in the morning, then they journeyed: whether it was by day or by night that the cloud was taken up, they journeyed. Or whether it were two days, or a month, or a year, that the cloud tarried upon the tabernacle, remaining thereon, the children of Israel abode in their tents, and journeyed not: but when it was taken up, they journeyed."

The cloud that God had given to the children of Israel was the tool that God used to lead them. If God wanted them to stay still for awhile, then the cloud would not move. If God wanted them to move, then the cloud would move. There is one thing I want you to notice in this verse, God says whether it were two days, a month, or a year, the children of Israel were to follow the cloud.

Sometimes in life God does not always move as fast as we would like Him to move. There will be times in our lives when God moves quickly and then there will be times in our lives when God will choose to wait for awhile to move. During these times we cannot become impatient with God. We must realize that God has a purpose for everything, and this purpose is not always going to agree with our time schedule. We must learn to be patient with God.

If these people would have moved without the cloud, they would have left the presence of God. Imagine allowing our impatience to move us out of the presence of God. Yet, this is what happens many times to Christians. If we are not careful, our impatience with God's schedule will move us right out from underneath His presence.

Whatever you do, learn to wait on God knowing that God knows what is best for you. God knows when we need to move in life, and He knows when we need to sit still for awhile. We just need to trust God's omniscience. Be careful to let God guide you in life and not to become impatient and move yourself away from the presence of God. Many times I have seen people become impatient with God and move before God wanted them to, only to see them later regret their impatient move. God's timing of how fast we should move in our lives and in our ministries is always right; don't move faster than God.

Taking God's Blessings For Granted

Numbers 11:4-6
"And the mixt multitude that was among them fell a lusting: and the children of Israel also wept again, and said, Who shall give us flesh to eat? We remember the fish, which we did eat in Egypt freely; the cucumbers, and the melons, and the leeks, and the onions, and the garlick: But now our soul is dried away: there is nothing at all, beside this manna, before our eyes."

How sad it is to see the children of Israel complaining about the blessings of God which they experienced every morning. Imagine, every day they saw God's blessings come down from Heaven in the form of manna, and yet, they were complaining to Moses about the manna. What happened was they had manna so often that they began to take for granted what God was doing for them. They became used to the blessings of God.

How careful we as Christians need to be that we don't get tired of the blessings that God has given to us. How careful we should be that we don't take for granted the blessings of God. Christians need to be careful that they don't get so used to God's blessings that they begin to complain that God is not blessing them enough.

This happens over and over again among God's people. God has blessed us more than we could ever imagine and yet we start complaining that what God has given to us is not enough. How wicked this is! If we will look back at what we used to have, we will realize we have so much more now than we ever had before. We get so used to God's blessings that we forget to thank Him daily for those blessings. We should never let God's blessings get old. We need to thank God daily for His blessings so that we do not become like the children of Israel.

Everyday we ought to stop and think about how great God's blessings are. If we would daily remember them, I imagine we would have a hard time getting used to His blessings. Whatever you do, don't get used to God's blessings. Remember, as Jeremiah did in the book of Lamentations, God's mercies are new every morning.

Don't Get Dirty

Numbers 19:22
"And whatsoever the unclean person toucheth shall be unclean; and the soul that toucheth it shall be unclean until even."

How important it is for people to be careful with whom they come in contact. We see in this verse that the unclean person causes a clean person to become unclean. Just by the touch of the unclean person the clean person becomes unclean.

This is why it is so important who we let touch us in life. When I say touch us, I am not talking of someone physically touching us. I am talking of a person touching us through their influence. For instance, I must be careful about letting Hollywood touch me through their movies. When they touch me through their movies, I become what they are. When I let unclean books touch me, books with bad language and pictures, then I become what these books are. Whatever touches me in my life I become. Just the touch of something unclean will cause me to be unclean. So, I must be careful about what touches me. We can all be touched in several ways. I am touched through the things I see, hear and the people I talk to and run with. Let me briefly deal with each of these.

First, I must be careful with what I see and read. The books I read, and I am even talking about religious books, I will become. Yes, we need to be careful about what we watch on television, but we also need to be careful about the books we read. Don't read books by authors who don't believe like we believe.

Second, I must be careful about what I listen to. Don't listen to the music of worldly people. Don't listen to preachers and teachers who don't believe like us. Don't go to schools where teachers don't believe the Bible. In each of these instances, when I listen to these people, I am letting them touch my mind and influence me. Their touch will cause me to eventually become unclean.

Third, be careful with whom you spend time. You are becoming like those with whom you spend time. Each of us must be careful of our circle of friends and acquaintances. Each person we talk to and each person we spend time with is influencing us in some way.

Just remember, all it takes is being touched by someone who is unclean, and once you are touched, you are unclean. If you want to stay clean then don't get around people and things that are dirty. Every month you should go over each of these areas and determine to clean up some things in your life.

3 Steps To Compromise

Number 25:1-3
"And Israel abode in Shittim, and the people began to commit whoredom with the daughters of Moab. And they called the people unto the sacrifices of their gods: and the people did eat, and bowed down to their gods. And Israel joined himself unto Baalpeor: and the anger of the LORD was kindled against Israel."

The attack of the world against God's people is an ongoing battle. Here in the story of Balaam and the Midianites, the Midianites were not able to destroy God's people through battle, so they tried the next best thing to destroy God's people; compromise. You will notice the path they took to destroy God's people is the same path that we must guard against today. The three-step path that led to God's anger against Israel is the same path that the world tries to get us to take everyday.

First, they try to get us to marry their sons and daughters. How careful we must be in the area of whom we let our children date. If our children date the lost world or even date a liberal Christian, they will eventually forsake God. This is what happened in this story. This is why we must be careful about what activities we attend. If we attend activities with the world then our children will marry children from the world.

Second, they try to get us to come to their religious services. If nothing epitomizes America more than these two verses, then I don't know what does. The world and the liberals all try to get us to think that we are all serving the same God, but we are just doing it in different ways. Well I have news for you, we are not all serving the same God! We serve Jehovah God, Who is a jealous God. Jehovah God is not the same as Muhammad or Buddha or even the god of the liberal who is not virgin born. This is why we must not go to the religious functions of the world, for this is all a part of their method of destroying us.

Third, we see the people forsake the LORD and join Baal-peor. This is always the final step. If America is not careful, and we are not far from this, then America will no longer serve Jehovah God. When this happens it will bring the wrath of God upon our land.

This is why we need preachers and Christians alike to sound the truth aloud. This is why we need people to stop joining up with the world and with the "religious people" of our society. Let us stay with our own kind and serve God the way God wants us to serve Him. Let us look at ourselves daily and make sure that we are not taking any of these steps so that we do not become guilty of turning ourselves and our country away from God.

The Message Of Rebellion

Number 27:12-14
"And the LORD said unto Moses, Get thee up into this mount Abarim, and see the land which I have given unto the children of Israel. And when thou hast seen it, thou also shalt be gathered unto thy people, as Aaron thy brother was gathered. For ye rebelled against my commandment in the desert of Zin, in the strife of the congregation, to sanctify me at the water before their eyes: that is the water of Meribah in Kadesh in the wilderness of Zin."

One of the reasons why rebellion against God is so bad is because of the message it preaches to the heathen. When a Christian rebels against God they are challenging the Deity and power of God. Notice in verse twenty-four what God said Moses' rebellion did; it failed to sanctify God in the eyes of the people. Not only was this rebellion of Moses a sin in itself because he directly disobeyed God, but it also hurt God in the eyes of the people. His rebellion against God no doubt caused people to continue to disobey God in certain areas of their lives.

Rebellion always hurts other people. We do not know, and will probably never know, who our rebellion is affecting. We can rest assured when we rebel against God, we are not just hurting ourselves, we are also hurting others and we are hurting the cause of Christ. People watch us, and when they see us directly disobey God we are telling them that it is ok to make our own decisions, even if these decisions go against what God tells us to do. Every Christian needs to be careful to obey everything that God tells them to do. We need to be careful that we do not lead someone astray because of our rebellion.

Rebellion has nothing to do with someone being a maverick. Rebellion has nothing to do with us "being our own man." Rebellion has nothing to do with us standing up for our own rights. Rebellion is all about us getting our own way.

Rebellion hurts us, God and those whom we influence. No matter what the cause of our rebellion, it is never justified.

Even though Moses was angry with the people, his rebellion was not justified. Moses' rebellion was wrong because he disobeyed God. Instead of being a people who rebel against God, let us be a people who are sensitive to the voice of God and who do what He asks us to do so that we will help and not hurt His cause.

No Justification For Wrong

Deuteronomy 1:26-27
"Notwithstanding ye would not go up, but rebelled against the commandment of the LORD your God: And ye murmured in your tents, and said, Because the LORD hated us, he hath brought us forth out of the land of Egypt, to deliver us into the hand of the Amorites, to destroy us."

What a wicked statement the people of God made in this verse to justify their rebellion against the commandment of the LORD. The justification of their rebellion against God was that God brought them into the wilderness because He hated them. Now think of how foolish and ludicrous this statement is. God chose them out of all the countries of the earth to be His people, and He hated them? God stood up against Pharaoh in the land of Egypt to deliver them from him, and He hated them? God gave them manna from Heaven every day for food to eat, and He hated them? God gave them shelter from the heat and the cold, and He hated them? God spoke to them audibly from Heaven like He had spoken to no other country or people before or since, and He hated them? On and on we could go to explain what God did for Israel because He loved them and because they were His chosen people. Now for them to say that God hated them so they could justify rebelling against His commandments was nothing more than a poor excuse.

Yet, over and over again Christians constantly come up with poor excuses as to why they do wrong. We all can, if we really wanted to, come up with poor excuses of why we want to rebel against God's commandments. We could all justify why we do wrong, but our justification is simply an excuse.

We must be careful that we do not justify our rebellion against God by placing the blame on God and what He supposedly has not done for us. Always remember, there is no justifiable reason to do wrong; especially blaming God.

Instead of blaming God for why we do wrong, why not stand up to our wrong and accept our responsibility. If we will do this, then God will be more willing to help us. As long as we try to justify our wrong, we are only stirring the wrath of God against us. Don't be a person who tries to justify your wrong with foolish excuses. Be a person who faces the wrong that you have done and get it right so that you can move on and have God's blessings again.

Sin Is Not A Game

Deuteronomy 7:25-26

"The graven images of their gods shall ye burn with fire: thou shalt not desire the silver or gold that is on them, nor take it unto thee, lest thou be snared therein: for it is an abomination to the LORD thy God. Neither shalt thou bring an abomination into thine house, lest thou be a cursed thing like it: but thou shalt utterly detest it, and thou shalt utterly abhor it; for it is a cursed thing."

In my home, when I was a boy, we were never allowed to play like we were doing something that was wrong. For instance, candy cigarettes were popular when I was young. It seemed like every child in the church was allowed to have candy cigarettes. Well, that was every child but four, our family. I can remember telling my mother that they were only candy. Then she would remind me that in our house we don't play like we are doing wrong. She told me sin is never funny, and sin will never be imitated in our house. Though everyone in the church thought my parents were too strict, they were right.

That is exactly what God was trying to teach His people in these verses. God was giving instructions to Israel on what to do when they conquered a city or a country. He promised them that they would conquer the land of Canaan, but God was concerned that His people, if they were not careful, would take up other gods. What God told Israel to do was to destroy all the idols that these lands worshiped. He even said that if the idols were made of silver and gold, they were not to take the silver and gold home. God did not want any resemblance of these gods in the homes of His people. He did not want anything that would be a reminder of other gods in their homes.

For what purpose was God doing this? God did this because He did not want this gold and silver to tempt them to worship these gods. You will notice that God said, *"...lest*

133

thou be snared therein…" God knew, if they let the grounded gold and silver from these idols in their houses, that the Devil would use this to tempt the children of Israel. God was trying to keep His people away from any temptation.

We must learn from this that sin is not a game. We must never let any resemblance of sin in our homes. Parents, never let your children play like they are doing wrong. It is never funny when children play like they are dancing. If dancing is wrong then why play like you are dancing? If we let our children imitate sin, then eventually that imitation will become reality. I have learned in life, if you never imitate something you have less chance of doing it.

Let us watch ourselves and our children so that we don't find ourselves thinking that sin is a game. Let us be careful to never let any resemblance of sin in our homes. For any resemblance of sin can become a snare to us and can eventually become our downfall. Let us follow the warning of God to completely destroy all imitation of sin in our homes. Remember, sin is not a game!

Dealing With Sin

Deuteronomy 9:3
"Understand therefore this day, that the LORD thy God is he which goeth over before thee; as a consuming fire he shall destroy them, and he shall bring them down before thy face: so shalt thou drive them out, and destroy them quickly, as the LORD hath said unto thee."

Sin is something that must be dealt with swiftly and firmly. You will notice that when God told the Israelites to destroy the Anakims, they were to do this quickly. You will also notice that He did not say just drive them out and let them go free; He said He wanted them to be completely destroyed.

First, when you are facing giants of sin in your life, the only way to get victory over these sins is to quickly deal with them. You will never overcome sin when you let it hang around for awhile. Sin must be dealt with quickly.

Secondly, when dealing with sin, you must destroy sin. Do not deal with sin gently, for it controls you. You must destroy everything about sin. You cannot give any place to sin.

There is one last thing I want you to notice about sin. Only God can give you the victory over sin. Notice in this verse that God reminds the people that He is *"...a consuming fire."* The reason He reminded them of this is because it is only through God that we can overcome the giant sins in our lives. We cannot overcome sin by ourselves. We can only overcome sin through God. If you fight the giants of sin by yourself, you will lose.

In fighting the giants of sin, I want you to remember two ways David fought giants. The first way he fought giants was through the strength of God's help. Secondly, when David fought the other four giants, he had to have help from others.

Giant sins can never be defeated alone; you must do it with God's help. Sometimes, you not only need the help of God to defeat giant sins, but God also wants you to get help from others to defeat these giant sins. When fighting sin, get God's help, but also employ the help of someone you can trust to help you to fight sin. Find someone whom you can become accountable to, and someone who will stay on you about overcoming your sin.

Without dealing with sin in these ways, you will never overcome the giant sins in your life. Dealing with sin in these ways will help you to overcome those giants.

The Responsibility Of The Preacher And The People

Deuteronomy 18:18-19
"I will raise them up a Prophet from among their brethren, like unto thee, and will put my words in his mouth; and he shall speak unto them all that I shall command him. And it shall come to pass, that whosoever will not hearken unto my words which he shall speak in my name, I will require it of him."

If a church is doing what it is supposed to do, then that church will produce preachers who will go out and pastor a church somewhere else. Every once in awhile a preacher boy will get to pastor the church in which he was raised. What a privilege it is to pastor one's home church. But for any man of God, what a privilege it is to get to pastor a people whom God has given him to feed and love. What a great responsibility! The responsibility does not only belong to the man of God, the responsibility is also that of the people who have the privilege of having a man of God in their midst.

God says in this verse that He would raise up a prophet among the people. That means that this prophet would have grown up with these people. This prophet would have been a close friend to some, a student of many teachers, a child of his parents and a neighborhood boy to many. In all of these instances, they must realize that when God anointed him, he became a prophet of God. In these verses, God show us the responsibility of the man of God and the people of God towards each other.

The responsibility of the man of God is to speak God's Words to the people. It matters not to whom these words are directed, he is to speak these words because this is his responsibility. He is not to speak anything that God has not said. That would mean no preacher should preach anything but the Word of God. He is not to preach preference; he is to preach the Word of God. He is not to preach his opinion; he is to preach the Word of God. He is not to preach what he wants; he is to preach the Word of God. Every man of God has an obligation to only preach what is found in the Word of God.

Just like the man of God has a responsibility to preach the Word of God, the people have a responsibility to listen to the Word of God. Notice they are to *"hearken unto"* God's Words spoken by the man of God. This means, this prophet may have grown up underneath you, but you are to listen to him as he preaches God's Word. He is no longer that boy in the neighborhood, he is a man of God and you are to listen to him. He is no longer whatever he was to you in the past, he is a man of God and you have a responsibility to listen to him and do what he preaches.

There is one more responsibility of the listener and that is, if the man of God starts preaching things that are not found in the Word of God or go directly against the Word of God, then the responsibility of the people is to leave that man of God. This would mean, when you have a pastor who is preaching against the Word of God, you as a listener have a responsibility to approach that man of God about his error. If he does not listen and the rest of the church will do nothing about this, then you should leave the church. I am not for splitting a church, but when a preacher is preaching things that are in direct contradiction to God's Word, you must do something about it. You are just as guilty as he is if you stay in that church.

Here is the question every man of God and church member must ask themselves, are we fulfilling the responsibilities that God has given to us? Let us be sure to preach what God commands us, whether or not it is popular among man. Let us also fulfill our responsibility in listening to the man of God, for in doing so we bring God's blessings upon our church and our lives.

Borrowing And Lending

Deuteronomy 24:10-11
"And when thou dost lend thy brother any thing, thou shalt not go into his house to fetch his pledge. Thou shalt stand abroad, and the man to whom thou dost lend shall bring out the pledge abroad unto thee."

When it came to borrowing and lending among the Israelites, God was very adamant about how it should be done. You will find earlier in the book of Deuteronomy God commanded the people when lending to each other to not charge a fee. God uses the word *"usury"* in the Bible as a term for charging fees. Many times it will be described by some as charging interest on a loan, but that is not what God was talking about. He was talking about charging fees on top of the interest.

Then we see God teach us in these verses how we are to collect that which is owed to us. Notice God says that the one who is owed the money is not to go inside the house of the one who owes the money. God wanted the home to be a peaceful place, a place for the family to feel safe from any outside source threatening them. So when a person was owed money, they were to deal with each other outside the home. The one who owed the money was to bring the money owed outside and pay his debt. Simply put, God did not want the one who was owed the money to go to the debtors' house to collect the debt. He wanted the one who owed the money to have the character to pay the debt. I believe the reason why God has these laws concerning borrowing and lending is to teach us some lessons.

First, God wanted us to be careful about lending our money out to anyone. God is not against a person making money. When you study the Bible, you will see that God believes in making money, but God was trying to keep people from becoming greedy and dishonest with each other in their business dealings. I believe though, the biggest reason why

God put these restrictions on lending money was because He wanted to protect His people from getting into big amounts of debt. If people realized that there was not much money in lending, then they most likely would not lend too often. God knew this, so this is why He put these restrictions on the lender. God would rather a person have the money up front to pay for something than for them to go out and borrow the money. It was all about keeping His people from going into debt.

Secondly, God wanted His people to think before borrowing. Many of these restrictions were there to make it hard to find someone who would loan money. This was because God wanted people to be careful about buying now and later trying to figure out a way to pay the debt. All of us must be careful about borrowing money. I am not saying it is wrong; it is just that we must be careful about the mentality of buying now and paying later. It is always better to live the principle: if you don't have it don't spend it.

All of us need to be careful about lending money to people and borrowing on a whim. If you are going to loan money, be sure that the person you are lending to truly needs what they are borrowing the money for. Be fair in your lending practices, and don't be extravagant in your fees. If you are going to borrow, wait a bit before borrowing to be sure you truly need what you think you need. When you do borrow, be sure to pay back what you owe.

And All The People Said...

Deuteronomy 27:26
"Cursed be he that confirmeth not all the words of this law to do them. And all the people shall say, Amen."

Twelve times in this chapter we see the phrase, *"And all the people shall say, Amen."* Now there is a reason why God allowed something to be said twelve times. Anytime God says something in the Bible, it is always to be listened to and obeyed. When God says something two times, I believe God is trying to get us to pay close attention to something He is trying to get across. When God says something three times, God wants us to see the importance of something so that we don't forget it. But, when God says something twelve times exactly the same way, and especially in the same chapter, then I think it is of the utmost importance that we listen and pay attention to whatever God is saying. God is trying to get our attention so we will do what He is talking about. This is the case with this phrase in this chapter.

Yes, God wanted His people to listen to the curses of what He is against, but God wanted something more from these people than just listening to the curses. God wanted His people to respond during the giving of these curses. When it is said twelve times, *"And all the people shall say, Amen,"* it is like a preacher who is preaching a sermon and makes this same statement for the people to respond to what he is saying. This is what God was doing to His people, and He was trying to teach us to do the same.

God not only wants us to listen to the preaching while the preacher is preaching, but God also wants us to say "Amen" when the preacher is preaching. If twelve times God said this phrase trying to get us to say "Amen," then I would think we ought to say "Amen" during the preaching time.

As I preach in churches nearly every week, I am amazed at how dead most people are during the preaching

141

time. Not only does God want you to listen to the preaching, but He also wants you to respond to what is being said during the preaching time. This is of the utmost importance to God. We have let certain groups in Christianity scare us away from showing emotion in our church services. God's people need to get away from the orthodoxy of our dead services and once again get some life during the preaching time. Men need to start saying "Amen" during the preaching time.

The next time you go to church, why don't you decide to get involved in the preaching time by saying "Amen." Don't be the one who has to get the preacher to prod you to say "Amen," but be the one who is already responding during the preaching time.

If God was to come and preach in our churches and say, *"And all the people shall say,"* would "Amen" already have been said, or would you be silent? Let's all say "Amen" before the preacher has to ask us to say "Amen."

Heads Or Tails

Deuteronomy 28:13
"And the LORD shall make thee the head, and not the tail; and thou shalt be above only, and thou shalt not be beneath; if that thou hearken unto the commandments of the LORD thy God, which I command thee this day, to observe and to do them:"

If you were to go to the bookstore in your town, you would find that there are a whole host of books on leadership setting on the shelves. It seems as if everybody and their brother have written a book on leadership. I am not against this, but the greatest book on leadership is the Bible. Who better to tell you how to be a leader than God? I wonder when was the last time someone picked up the Bible and read It so they could learn how to be a leader?

All throughout the Bible we find lessons on leadership. This is the case with this verse. God in this verse is teaching us how to be a leader of leaders. Notice the phrase, *"And the LORD shall make thee the head, and not the tail."* God was showing His people how they could be a leader of nations. He told them if they wanted to be a leader of nations then all they had to do was *"...hearken unto the commandments of the LORD."* I know this sounds simple, but this is truly the answer to being a leader of leaders. There are those in life who lead people; these are leaders. These people are most likely very good people as well. Then there are people who lead the leaders; these are leader of leaders.

God not only wants His people to be leaders, but He wants His people to be the leader of the leaders. He wants His people to be the ones who show the leaders how to live and react. God says the only way to be a leader of leaders is to listen to the commandments of God and to observe, or do the commandments of God.

If you want to be a leader of leaders, my suggestion would be to first of all, listen to God's commandments. This comes by reading the Bible everyday and by listening to the preacher when he preaches. Reading your Bible everyday will give you insights into life that others will never see and will propel you to become a leader. But just reading the Bible and listening to the preaching is not good enough, you also must do what the Bible tells you to do and what the preacher tells you to do.

Are you the head, the one who is the leader of leaders, or are you the tail, the follower of the leader of leaders? There is nothing wrong with being a follower, someone has to do this, but God's intention for His people is to be leaders of leaders. The only way to do this is to listen to and obey the commandments of God.

The Power Of Music

Deuteronomy 31:19-21
"Now therefore write ye this song for you, and teach it the children of Israel: put it in their mouths, that this song may be a witness for me against the children of Israel. For when I shall have brought them into the land which I sware unto their fathers, that floweth with milk and honey; and they shall have eaten and filled themselves, and waxen fat; then will they turn unto other gods, and serve them, and provoke me, and break my covenant. And it shall come to pass, when many evils and troubles are befallen them, that this song shall testify against them as a witness; for it shall not be forgotten out of the mouths of their seed: for I know their imagination which they go about, even now, before I have brought them into the land which I sware."

Music is a very powerful tool that God has given to us to use in His service. One of the most controversial subjects in Christianity is the subject of music. The range of what is right and wrong in music I will not discuss, but the power of music is clearly seen in these verses.

As Moses came to the end of his life, God commanded him to write a song to teach the children of Israel what God had done for them. God wanted Moses and the people of Israel to teach their children this song, so when the days came that they were in bondage because of their sins, this song would remind them of what God had done for them in the past. God knew that if they learned a song that it would never leave them as long as they lived.

Let me give you some thoughts concerning music that I believe we all need to remember. First, be very careful that you listen to the right kind of music all the time. How often do you walk through a store and hear a song from your past and find yourself humming the song even if the song was a bad song? This is why it is so important we listen to the right kind of music, for once a song is learned it will never be forgotten.

145

Second, we should repeatedly play good music for our children. So many times I find myself driving down the road singing a song I learned as a child because of the music that was played in our home. We were not a family that constantly tried to find new music, though I am not totally against this. We heard many of the same songs over and over again which reinforced in my mind the truths those songs were teaching. I believe we should sing good songs repeatedly in our churches and in our homes. We should be sure to play good music in our home over and over again so our children will have the truths of that music planted in their mind.

Third, be a person who sings constantly. The right music being played and sung will lift your spirit. Find a good song to sing for each day and make that your theme song and sing or whistle it throughout the day. Many times when I travel, I find myself in the elevator whistling or humming a song which normally gets a response from others commenting about how happy I seem to be. What an opportunity this opens up for people to hear the Gospel of Christ.

Lastly, let everyone of us look at our music and make sure it is the music God would want us to listen to. Realizing the power of music, we should constantly make sure that what we listen to is the right kind of music, for this music once learned, will never be forgotten by us or our children.

A Father's Responsibility

Joshua 4:5-7
"And Joshua said unto them, Pass over before the ark of the LORD your God into the midst of Jordan, and take ye up every man of you a stone upon his shoulder, according unto the number of the tribes of the children of Israel: That this may be a sign among you, that when your children ask their fathers in time to come, saying, What mean ye by these stones? Then ye shall answer them, That the waters of Jordan were cut off before the ark of the covenant of the LORD; when it passed over Jordan, the waters of Jordan were cut off: and these stones shall be for a memorial unto the children of Israel for ever."

I live in the Shenandoah Valley which is full of history from the American Revolution to the Civil War. Washington, D.C. is not far from where I live. All around us there are memorials that are set up that tell stories of what happened in the past. They do more than just tell us a story, they are also there to teach us about where we came from and what we should continue in the future.

As the children of Israel passed over the Jordan River, God commanded Joshua to have twelve men each take up a large stone out of the river and set those stones up as a memorial for them. These stones were there so that in the future when a father and son were walking along the banks of the river the son would see this pile of rocks and would ask his father what the memorial was all about. You see, every memorial has a story behind it. God gave the father a great responsibility to use these stones to teach generations to come what God had done for His people.

There are several lessons that we should learn from this story. First, we should be sure to set up memorials for generations to come. This generation should do something so that the next generation can see the power of God working in our lives. It is the responsibility of parents to get God to do a great work in their lives.

Second, we should look to the past to learn what to do in the present. Notice these stones were there to remind those in the present what God had done in the past. One of the greatest weaknesses of our society right now is that we have completely forsaken the past. The past should be a teacher to the present. If we stop learning from the past, we will destroy the present day in which we live. The past is a great teacher of what we should and should not do in the present.

Third, it is the responsibility of parents to teach their children about the works of God. Every parent should realize that they should use every opportunity to teach their children about the great works of God. Parents, don't leave it up to the church or the school to teach your children our history. You need to be the one to teach your children about where we came from in America and also as Christians. That means parents need to spend time learning about the past.

Lastly, let us never move the stones of history to make it politically correct today. In this present day, I see how we tend to be changing history to make it politically correct. We change it to fit our life styles so that we can justify how we are living. We need to leave the stones right where they are! Don't change the meaning of the past to justify how you are living today. Tell it exactly like it is. History unchanged can teach us a lot about how to live today.

Let us be careful to fulfill our responsibilities of teaching others our history without changing it so that we can keep what we were and who we are the same.

No Day Like This Day

Joshua 10:12-14
"Then spake Joshua to the LORD in the day when the LORD delivered up the Amorites before the children of Israel, and he said in the sight of Israel, Sun, stand thou still upon Gibeon; and thou, Moon, in the valley of Ajalon. And the sun stood still, and the moon stayed, until the people had avenged themselves upon their enemies. Is not this written in the book of Jasher? So the sun stood still in the midst of heaven, and hasted not to go down about a whole day. And there was no day like that before it or after it, that the LORD hearkened unto the voice of a man: for the LORD fought for Israel."

What a contrast this war was with the war of Ai. In the war of Ai, the LORD fought against Israel because of sin and in this war the LORD fought for Israel. As they fought the war at Gibeon, God did great things for them because He was on their side. Notice our text says *"...there was no day like that before it or after it..."* When God starts fighting for you, you will find that miraculous things begin to happen in your life.

This is one of the problems we see in Christianity today. We see people who are doing things on their own when what they need to do is get God to start fighting their battles for them. When God fights your battles, there will be days that you have never seen and will never see again because of the miracles of God.

What battles are you fighting today? I know you have one because everybody has battles. Are you fighting a battle to keep your marriage together? Get God involved in the battle and you will see miraculous things happen in your marriage. Are you fighting a battle with your children to keep them from doing wrong or to keep them from running with the wrong crowd? Your answer for a miracle in your children's lives is to get God to fight the battle for you. Are you fighting a battle with your finances to keep from going under? Whatever

149

your battle, God is the only answer to your battle. You must get God to fight for you.

You say, "How do we get God to fight for us?" You must ask God to fight the battles for you the same way Israel did in the battles that they fought. Everyday ask God to fight the battles for you, and beg Him to get involved. Then, stop trying your own methods of fighting these battles and depend on the methods of God.

Finally, get His wisdom to fight these battles by reading the Bible and asking Him for His wisdom. When this is done, be ready for Him to do something great for you in regard to your battles. If you are patient with God, before the sun sets on your battle, God will step in and do great things for you so that you will be able to say, "There is no day like this day, because God fought the battle for me." Stop fighting your battles yourself, and get God involved in the battles with you!

Satan Always Has Counterfeits

Psalm 115:2-3
Wherefore should the heathen say, Where is now their God? But our God is in the heavens: he hath done whatsoever he hath pleased."

A counterfeit will never give you what the original can give. This is why it is a counterfeit. The word *"counterfeit"* means it is "an imitation or a forgery of the original." In other words, a counterfeit only tries to imitate what the original truly is, but it is worthless simply because it is a counterfeit.

We see in this Psalm that the heathen ask the question, *"Where is now their God?"* to God's people. It is interesting that the answer is immediately given that *"our God is in the heavens."* In other words, our God is not limited to one place as are the idols of the heathen. This verse is actually teaching us the omnipresence of God and how that God can be and is everywhere all the time. As we continue in this Psalm, we see the heathen's idols have the shape of God, but they don't respond. Notice, it says these idols have a mouth, but the mouth will not speak. They have ears, but those ears do not hear. They have hands and feet, but they cannot walk or handle things. They even made their idols to have a throat, but the idols could not speak.

Herein lies the problem with the counterfeits of Satan, they may promise a lot, but they cannot produce what they promise, because they are counterfeits. Praise the Lord, we serve a God who can respond, and speak, and hear, and walk and handle us. We don't serve a dead God, we serve a living God!

We must learn something about Satan; he is a great counterfeiter. Whatever God has for us, Satan will make a counterfeit for us as well. The only difference is that the counterfeit cannot produce what it says it will. For instance, God gave us a church, but Satan also has churches out there.

This is why we must be careful to attend a church that preaches and lives what the Bible says. God gave us a family, but Satan has also offered us his counterfeit for a family as we see today with the sodomite households. These families just will not work for they are against God's methods. God has music for us to listen to, but Satan has also produced counterfeit music through the Christian rock and the music of the world. God gave us a Bible in the King James Bible 1611, but Satan has also offered us his counterfeits through all the other versions that have been produced. No matter what God offers us, Satan will always have a counterfeit.

Everyday we must be sure that we don't accept the counterfeits of Satan. I ask you, is there some counterfeit that Satan has offered you that you have accepted and are trying to use? Let me just be frank with you, it will never give you what it promises. O, at the beginning it may seem to satisfy, but once you put the counterfeit to the test, it will always fail. Only accept what God offers to you, and never accept the counterfeits of Satan.

The Most Dangerous Time Of Life

Joshua 11:23
"So Joshua took the whole land, according to all that the LORD said unto Moses; and Joshua gave it for an inheritance unto Israel according to their divisions by their tribes. And the land rested from war."

I need you to follow me in order to understand from where I am coming. For forty years the children of Israel had wandered in the wilderness facing trial after trial. Before the wilderness, they had faced over four hundred years of bondage in the land of Egypt. Since they had been in the land of Canaan, they had been at war for nearly a year. After all of these years, we see they finally have rest from war and bondage. Our text says, *"And the land rested from war."* This now became a very dangerous time for Israel. If they were not careful, their time of rest could have become a time of backsliding because they thought they had finally arrived. This is exactly what happened to them.

Every Christian must be very careful when they are not facing battles, not to allow themselves to backslide. Most of us are in some sort of battle all the time. Whether these battles we face are of our own doing or due to trials that are meant to strengthen us, most of us are constantly in some sort of battle.

Once in awhile, God gives us a reprieve from the battles of life to help us catch our breath. In these times of peace in our lives, we must watch ourselves because this can become a very dangerous time. Dangerous because we are not as careful about sin as when we are in battle. Dangerous because we don't pray as much as we would when in the battles. Dangerous because we don't read our Bibles as we would if we were in battles. Dangerous because we stop growing spiritually as battles force us to grow.

During these times of peace in our lives, we must watch ourselves in each of these areas so that we do not let them slip. We must guard ourselves so that we don't let sin creep in. We must be sure that we pray and read our Bible as much, if not more, than we would when in the battle. We must make sure that we don't get at ease and stop growing.

Enjoy the times of rest that God gives to you, but be very careful as the time of rest is a very dangerous time in your life. Don't let the Devil destroy you during your time of rest. Keep fighting sin, keep praying God's power down and gaining His wisdom through the Word of God. Instead of letting up and doing nothing, use the time of rest to grow more for the Lord. The time of rest is not the time to stop growing; the time of rest is a time to conquer even more.

I Love The LORD Because...

Psalm 116:1
"I love the LORD, because he hath heard my voice and my supplications."

The psalmist does something in this verse that every Christian ought to do periodically in their life. The psalmist sits down and writes why he loves the LORD. He has many reasons for loving the LORD. He mentions the reason why He loves God is because God heard his prayer, He helped him in time of death and He was gracious and merciful to him. The LORD was so many things to the psalmist that he thought it would only be right to write out why He loved the LORD.

I believe one of the reasons why Christians struggle so much in their Christian lives is because they never take time to sit down and write out why they love the LORD. Every week you should sit down, get a piece of paper out and write down every reason why you love the LORD. I am very serious about doing everything I just said. Too many times we just say that we will go through these things in our mind, and this is fine, but I believe taking time to write these reasons out will help us to think through these things in a greater way. Not only does it force us to take time to think of why we love the LORD, but it also shows us how many reasons we have to love the LORD. It can almost become convicting to us when we look at the little list that we come up with.

You will notice though, that the love in this psalm is all because of what the LORD had done for the psalmist. This type of love is merely a kindergarten type of love, for it is a love based on what He has done for us. This type of love, when hard times come, begins to blame God and say that God does not love us. What a shallow love we have if our love is only because of what He has done for us.

Yet, there is a greater love that I believe we should have for the LORD. The greater love I am talking about and

155

that I believe God desires from every Christian is to love God, not for what He has done for us, but for Who He is. May we work toward the type of love where we love God, not only for what He has given and done for us, but may we love Him for just being Who He is; God!

There is only one way you will get this type of love. Do what I previously stated and sit down and write out why you love the LORD on a regular basis.

Why don't you take some time out of your schedule today and write down why you love the LORD. Could you come up with a page full of reasons why you love the LORD? Try it and see what you can come up with. Simply write, "I love the LORD because..." and then write the many reasons why you love the LORD. When you are done then grade your love for the LORD to determine whether your love for the LORD is still in kindergarten or in graduate school.

Because Of You

Joshua 23:2-3
"And Joshua called for all Israel, and for their elders, and for their heads, and for their judges, and for their officers, and said unto them, I am old and stricken in age: And ye have seen all that the LORD your God hath done unto all these nations because of you; for the LORD your God is he that hath fought for you."

At the end of Joshua's life he called all the leaders of Israel together to remind them of all the works that God had done for Israel. He reminded them that God had conquered the nations of the land in which they dwell. As you go through this whole chapter, you will see that Joshua reminds the people of the promises that God fulfilled.

The key phrase that made all of this possible is seen in this verse, *"...because of you."* It was only because of the people that the lands were conquered. It was only because of the people that they saw the great works of God. It was only because of the people that God was able to show His mighty works. God used people to do the mighty works that He had promised.

Let me remind you today that God still uses people. What Christian would not want to see God do mighty works today? Well let me remind you, God wants to do mighty works, but He uses people to do His mighty works. I wonder how many mighty works have not been done by God because there was no one He could find through which to do His mighty works. Yes, God could do them without us, but He chooses to use people to do His mighty works.

You see, it is because of you that God can help other people. It is because of you God can comfort those with hurting hearts. It is because of you that God encourages a discouraged person. It is because of you that God can still build great churches. It is because of you that God can meet the needs of others. It is because of you that God can still save the lost soul from Hell. O, don't get me wrong, God can do all of this without us, but He uses people like you to do these great works.

It would be sad if no one is helped because you are too wrapped up in getting your own way. It would be sad that the needs of others are not met because you are too worried about getting your own way.

I ask you, how many people today are not being helped because of you? I ask you, how many great works of God are not being performed because you are too wrapped up in doing your own thing instead of the will of God? I could go on and on, but I think you understand what I am talking about.

Today, let us go out and let God's great works be seen because we are surrendered to letting God do something through us. Let us always keep in the forefront of our minds that it is because of us that God's great works are performed because He chose to use us to do these great works. Because of you, what great work is God going to do today?

Quickly Turned Out Of The Way

Judges 2:17
"And yet they would not hearken unto their judges, but they went a whoring after other gods, and bowed themselves unto them: they turned quickly out of the way which their fathers walked in, obeying the commandments of the LORD; but they did not so."

The children of Israel seemed to have a bad habit which they could not knock. We see in this verse that *"...they turned quickly out of the way which their fathers walked in."* We see here that it never took them long to turn from what they were taught. They were a people who never saw the importance of doing what they knew was right. According to this verse, God sent judges, or preachers, their way to try and get them to turn back, but the Bible states that they would not listen to them. How sad it is that the people of God were not afraid when they quickly turned away from the One Who had delivered them from Egypt and guided them into the Promised Land.

As I read this it brings me to ask you a question. Are you like the Israelites, a person who quickly turns away from that which you have been taught? To the one who has been raised in a Christian home, does it not matter what your parents have taught you, are you always looking for a way to quickly leave what you have been taught? I ask the one who has been in the church long enough to know better, are you always looking for a way to not do what you know has been preached from the Word of God?

Notice the reason why a person will quickly turn away from that which they have been taught. The reason why this happens is because people won't listen to the preaching. Those who will not *"hearken"* to the preaching are those who will quickly turn away from what is right.

There are some who read this to whom it matters not what the preacher says. You have already made up your mind and justify why you do what you do. You are the one who quickly turns out of the way. The preacher can tell you what to do and you always have an excuse as to why you cannot do it. You are the one who is quickly turning out of the way. He can warn you and plead with you not to do it, but you justify your reasoning not realizing that you are quickly turning from God's way.

There are some who just won't listen to the preacher. Your mind wanders when he preaches because you just don't want to be there. Watch out, you are on you way to turn quickly out of God's way.

Everyone needs to be careful to listen when the preacher is preaching. Let us not be a people who no matter what the preacher says, have our own reasoning as to why we are going to do something. Let us be a people who listen to the preaching realizing it is God that has sent that message to us.

Then, let us be careful not to make it a habit or routine to quickly turn from God's way; the way which we have been taught is right. Instead, let's be people who quickly turn back to God's way, realizing that His way always leads to happiness.

Faint, Yet Pursuing

Judges 8:4
"And Gideon came to Jordan, and passed over, he, and the three hundred men that were with him, faint, yet pursuing them."

Has there ever been a time in your Christian life when you felt as though you could not make it in some area? I mean, have you ever come to the point when you have just become weary of fighting and weary of trying and it seems like you just can't take another step?

The three hundred men who followed Gideon knew exactly how you feel. They had just fought the great battle against the Midianite army, and now they are pursuing the princes of Midian and their companies to try and destroy them. These three hundred men had just done the work that it would normally take thousands of men to do and now they are weary with this pursuit. I love what this verse says about these men, though these men were weary and tired the Bible states they were *"...faint, yet pursuing them."*

These great men who followed Gideon were not ordinary men as we see in the choosing of Gideon's army. These men were not ordinary in the way they drank water. They were not ordinary in the fact that, in the face of weariness, they still pursued and would not give up what they had started.

What encouragement this can be to all of us who face what seem to be insurmountable objects in life. What motivation this should give to every one who is becoming weary with pursuits that seem to never come to fruition. These men give us an example to follow. When we have become faint or weary in our pursuits of life, we must keep on pursuing until the job is done.

Have you become weary in your pursuits of life? Let me give you some encouragement to keep on pursuing until you accomplished what you set out to do. Are you weary in trying to rear your children right when it seems like everything is against you? Keep pursuing and don't give up, the day will come when you will look back and be glad you did not listen to your weariness. Are you weary in your marriage, and wonder how long it is going to take for things to get better? Keep pursuing and don't give up. It is those who don't give up who one day look back with joy and see what their marriage has become because they did not give up during the times when they were weary.

I do not know with what you have become weary with? Whatever the case and whatever the cause that you pursue, don't listen to the weariness that wants you to quit. Listen to the cause of what you are pursuing and keep going. It is when you feel like quitting that victory is almost there. I implore you to keep going though faint and weary; victory will come if you don't give up.

Love Is Stupid

Judges 16:4
"And it came to pass afterward, that he loved a woman in the valley of Sorek, whose name was Delilah."

A lot can be learned from the life of Samson about how and where to choose who to date and marry. We notice in this verse it says that Samson, *"...loved a woman...whose name was Delilah."* This may be one of the most tragic relationships we see in the Bible; the relationship between Samson and Delilah. Samson fell in love with this woman, but you will notice the Bible never states that she loved him. Delilah was a prostitute whom he had hired, and this is why she had no feelings for him.

The Philistines seeing they had an opportunity to kill their enemy, hired her to find out the secret of his strength. Here comes what I want you to notice, she asked him where his strength lay and every time he told her how to make him weak she would do it. Samson was so blinded by his love he literally let Delilah destroy him. How stupid love had made him. Delilah eventually destroyed him and all because he got himself involved in a wrong relationship.

I have always said that love does not make a person blind, love makes a person stupid. Let me give you several thoughts on finding and dating the right person.

First, go to the right places to find a person to marry and date. This is why it is so important for young people to stay in church or go to Bible College. You have a better chance of finding the right person in these places than you will at the bar or the movies. This is why parents need to send their children to the right schools. Your children will marry those with whom they attend school.

Second, give someone veto power in your dating life. Love makes a person stupid. Now don't get mad at me, but people will do stupid things when they are "in love." This is why you need someone with veto power so they can tell you what to do when you are blinded by your love.

Third, choose someone who runs with the right friends. Notice that Delilah was running with the enemies of Samson. We need to be sure that whomever we choose to date and marry does not have friends of which we would not approve. If they do, then you need to stop dating them.

Fourth, don't date someone who will use you for their own gain. You are dating the wrong person if they say, "If you love me, you will do this..." This happens most of the time with your purity. Anyone who truly loves you will not date you to see what they can get out of you or use you as a trophy piece.

Last, if your parents do not approve of whom you are dating then don't date them. Did you see in this story that Samson never told his parents? Why? Because he knew they would not approve. If you are trying to hide whom you are dating from the ones who love you the most, then something cannot be right. Those in a right relationship will not have to hide what they are doing.

Parents, keep a close eye on your children and whom they date. Teach your children these principles because the one thing that changes your life the most after salvation is the person whom you choose to marry. Let us all be very careful in this most important decision. This decision will change your life forever.

A Lesson In Decision Making

Ruth 4:5-6
"Then said Boaz, What day thou buyest the field of the hand of Naomi, thou must buy it also of Ruth the Moabitess, the wife of the dead, to raise up the name of the dead upon his inheritance. And the kinsman said, I cannot redeem it for myself, lest I mar mine own inheritance: redeem thou my right to thyself; for I cannot redeem it."

One of the mistakes we see people make, especially in our day and age, is they consider the here and now in their decision making and not to how their decision will affect them in the future.

In this part of the story of Boaz and Ruth, Ruth's husband had died, and according to the law, it was the responsibility of the next of kin to marry Ruth and raise up a child in the name of her deceased husband. Now the next of kin did have a right to decline to fulfill this responsibility if they wanted. This is where Boaz becomes so important to this story. Boaz goes to the next of kin to see if he is going to fulfill his responsibility in marrying Ruth and rear up a child in the name of the dead husband. This next of kin made a classic mistake by looking only at the immediate future and how he thought it would ruin his own name and inheritance, therefore he declined the offer. Because of this, Boaz now had the right to inherit all the land of the deceased and the right to marry Ruth.

Here is the part of the story I want you to notice, because this other kin looked at the immediate in his decision, he missed out on being in the lineage of Christ. Is it not interesting that everyone knows the name Boaz, but nobody knows the name of this next of kin? He was so worried about his name and reputation that he missed out on his name being remembered forever and all this because he was concerned about the present and did not look to the future.

165

When it comes to making decisions, you must never look at how the decision is going to affect you in the present. You must always look at how this decision is going to affect you in the future. One of the reasons our country is in the shape she is in is because many people vote on what a candidate is going to do for them right now instead of what the candidate will do for this country's future. This is the same reason why young people lose their purity. They look at the satisfaction of the immediate instead of taking into account the impact this decision will have on their future. Many adults go into deep debt because of the immediate satisfaction this possession will give them instead of looking down the road and seeing how they will have nothing when they are old if they continue to spend right now.

Every person, when making a decision, cannot look at the immediate benefit of a decision. Instead, base your decisions on what consequences they will carry in the long run. When you start looking at how the decision will benefit or affect you in the future, you will find yourself making better decisions.

I beg you to stop making decisions based on how it affects you now and start making decisions on what they will do for you in the future. If you will do this, you will find happiness and no regrets in the future.

Desire

Psalm 121:1
"I will lift up mine eyes unto the hills, from whence cometh my help."

Webster's 1828 dictionary defines the word "desire" as "the internal act, which, by influencing the will, makes us proceed to action." Desire is a very powerful tool that is needed in our society today.

The psalmist says in this verse, *"I will lift up mine eyes unto the hills..."* I want you to notice the first two words of this verse, *"I will."* Those two words tell us that the psalmist had desire. *"I will"* is a desire to do something. His desire influenced him to seek after God. His desire caused him to spring to action. This is what desire does.

Napoleon said, "Desire is the starting point of all achievement, not a hope, not a wish, but a keen pulsating desire which transcends everything." What this world needs is a good dose of desire pumped into the veins of every person.

Without desire you will never be successful. Desire is what makes a marriage work. Desire is what motivates a student to get good grades. Desire is what guides a person to achieve great things. Desire is what kept Jesus going to the cross. Desire is what takes a person out of the ghetto to accomplish great things in their life. Desire is what drives the unemployed to find employment. Desire is what keeps a sick person doing what they do not feel like doing. Desire is what drives you into action to do great things.

Too many people wish they had something and dream about having something, but have no desire to do something. For instance, many people wish they could lose weight, but only those who have a desire to lose weight will lose the weight. Many people wish and dream that they could improve

167

their lives, but only those with desire will improve their lives. I cannot stress enough the importance of having desire.

I ask you, are you wishing and dreaming for something in life or do you have a desire to do something in life? What you need to do is change your wish and dream into a desire and you will see yourself beginning to head towards the destination of your dream. Without desire you will continue to stay exactly where you are right now. Desire is the very foundation that will spring you into action to acquire what you have dreamed about for years. Desire is the only thing that will turn dreams into reality.

Why don't you today, instead of griping about what you don't have and wishing you could have something else, go to God and ask Him to place desire in your heart. Imagine how the dreams that you have could help your family and others, and you will find that desire will begin to come alive in your heart.

Children Can Serve The LORD Too

1 Samuel 3:1
"And the child Samuel ministered unto the LORD before Eli. And the word of the LORD was precious in those days; there was no open vision."

Never underestimate the importance of children serving the LORD. The Bible says, *"And the child Samuel ministered unto the LORD."* What I love about this is that Samuel did not wait until he was an adult to serve the LORD; he started serving the LORD as a child. I also admire his parents in this story for they did not try to stop him from serving the LORD. There is one other person that I respect in this story and that is Eli, the priest of the LORD. All of these worked together in Samuel serving God as a child.

Let me remind the children, parents and preachers, God wants children to serve Him. If God can get the heart of a child as a child, then God knows that they will have a better chance of serving Him as an adult. This is why we should not hold children back from serving the LORD. It is very important for us to understand that God wants children to serve Him.

Children, you are never too young to start serving the LORD. All throughout the Bible, God uses children to serve Him. He used a child to be king at eight years of age. He used a teenage boy to kill Goliath. He used a child's lunch to feed five thousand people. God uses children! Don't ever think you are too young to serve God.

Parents, don't you be guilty of holding your children back from serving God. If anything, you should create opportunities for your children to serve God. Why is it we think children are too young to serve God, but they are not too young to play sports? If a child can play sports, then a child can serve God. I thank God that my parents never held me back from serving God as a child. In fact, they encouraged me to serve God as a child as I think every parent should.

169

Lastly, preachers, don't you be guilty of not letting children serve God. Too many preachers create programs for children to play while the parents are serving God, and I believe this is wrong. Children need to learn how to serve God as well. Instead of creating programs for children to play, you ought to create programs for children to serve God.

Are you guilty of using the age of someone to hold them back from serving God? Let each of us remember that God uses children for His service. Let each of us encourage children to minister unto the LORD.

When Doing Right Brings Trouble

1 Samuel 7:7
"And when the Philistines heard that the children of Israel were gathered together to Mizpeh, the lords of the Philistines went up against Israel. And when the children of Israel heard it, they were afraid of the Philistines."

Has it ever seemed to you that whenever you make a decision to do right that bad seems to follow? You would think that as soon as you get right with God that God's blessings would immediately follow, but the opposite seems to happen.

This is what happened to God's people. Here Samuel preaches a sermon to Israel about returning back to God and putting away the strange gods that they had been worshiping. We see that the people listened to this great prophet, came together and put away all their heathen idols and worship practices. What a time of rejoicing this should have been, but instead we see that when the Philistines heard that God's people were gathered together, they came against the children of Israel to try to destroy them. This is Satan's tactic of discouraging us when we decide to quit sin.

Let me warn everyone, when you decide to put sin away and get right with God, Satan is not happy about this and he will fight you immediately. You will have to expect bad to follow when you start doing right. O, I know you would think that good should follow, but you must also realize that Satan is going to fight you. God will certainly bless you for doing right, but Satan will certainly fight you as well. Let me give you some tips to follow when you decide to start doing right in an area of your life.

First, when you lay aside sin, you did the right thing. Whether or not blessings follow immediately after doing right, you must take solace in the fact that you did right. You must never forget that you did the right thing.

171

Second, expect Satan to fight against you. If you will expect Satan to fight you immediately, then you have a better chance of not getting discouraged when the battles come. Battles are going to come whether you prepare yourself or not, so just expect them once you get right.

Third, God will bless you for doing right. God's blessings may not come immediately, but they will come. You must realize that because you started doing right you may not see God's blessings immediately just like you did not see God's punishment immediately when you started doing wrong. Now, God may send you a small blessing for doing right, but His great blessings for doing right will come in time.

Last of all, run to God and ask Him for help to deliver you from the attacks of Satan. Verse 8 says, *"Cease not to cry unto the LORD our God for us, that he will save us..."* Christian, when the attacks of Satan come against you for doing right, you need God's help. I beg of you to cease not to cry unto the LORD for His help in overcoming these attacks. God wants to bless you and He wants to help you, but you must be sure to ask Him for this help.

So, when we decide to do right, let us not become discouraged and quit doing right when the attacks of Satan come. Let us take courage and do what I have advised realizing that, in God's timing, our decision to do right will prove to be the right decision.

The Cause Of Deterioration

1 Samuel 13:19-20
"Now there was no smith found throughout all the land of Israel: for the Philistines said, Lest the Hebrews make them swords or spears: But all the Israelites went down to the Philistines, to sharpen every man his share, and his coulter, and his axe, and his mattock."

What is it that causes churches to go liberal? What is it that would cause movements to cease from being what they were originally? What is it that causes political parties to change from their original platform? What is it that causes people to change? I believe we see the cause of change in the story we read above.

One of the saddest statements we see in this verse is there was no smith found in all of Israel who could sharpen their swords or spears. Because there was no smith, the Israelites went to the Philistines, their enemy, to have them sharpen their swords and spears. The only problem with this is, if you go to war with them, they could destroy you by not allowing their smiths to sharpen your swords or spears. There are a couple of lessons we can learn from these verses that will help us, not only spiritually, but nationally as well.

First, we must not go to the liberals to learn how to build our churches. Why do we think we can stay conservative when we continue to run to the churches that have forsaken the methods and doctrines of the Word of God for our ideas? If we run to them to get ideas then we will end up becoming like them. This is why we MUST stay with our own kind so that we can keep ourselves from becoming like them.

Second, we must continue to produce preachers in our churches. The smith is like the preacher in that he is the one who helps Christians to keep their lives straight and sharp for the LORD. If we don't produce preachers then we will end up not having any *"smiths"* in our land. One of the greatest tragedies in our churches today is that we are not producing preachers. I believe the reason is because we have fallen for the trap of Satan in telling ourselves that we don't want to be the ones to call our children into the ministry. I can certainly agree with this, but we can set the bar high for our boys at home and church and let them know that we want them to become a preacher when they grow up. If we will do this, we will find our children aiming for this, for they will only strive to become what we set in front of them. This is what my parents did for me, and I am very glad they did.

Let me close by saying, deterioration is caused by not producing our own *"smiths."* Let us not go to the liberals to get our ideas, but let us instead rear preachers in our homes and churches who will continue to preach what we know is right so that our churches will stay pure and clean. Let us be sure that our homes are training grounds for servants of the LORD and not training grounds for worldly children. Let us be careful that in our churches we rear young people to become preachers and servants of the LORD instead of settling for them to just fill the pews.

A Step Between

1 Samuel 20:3
"And David sware moreover, and said, Thy father certainly knoweth that I have found grace in thine eyes; and he saith, Let not Jonathan know this, lest he be grieved: but truly as the LORD liveth, and as thy soul liveth, there is but a step between me and death."

The situation between Saul and David at the time this story happened is very serious. Saul had tried to kill David several times and now David feels as if death could be eminent. He is now fleeing for his life as Saul had once again tried to kill David with a javelin. Now David and his dear friend Jonathan, are having a conversation about David's situation when David says to Jonathan that *"...there is but a step between me and death."* David knew that life can change in a moments notice. He knew it would only take one bad move in his life and he would be dead. Only one step was between him and death.

Likewise, just as David was one step from death, let me say to everyone reading this that there is but one step between us and heartache. I try not to be negative, but we must be realistic in life and realize that every one of us have a step between us and heartache. I mean, there is only one step between us and death. There is only one step between us and sickness. There is only one step between us and financial hardships. There is only one step between us and a bad decision. There is but one step between each of us and hard times. There is but one step between us and a bad decision. What we are being taught is that life may be grand right now, but we must realize that we are all not far from a heartache that can change our lives. Therefore, we must be careful to avoid taking the wrong steps in life.

To many who read this, that step has already been taken. O, what a hard step to take, but it is a part of life. Let me remind you though, it is God who directs our steps. If God allowed hardship to come, it is only because God has a plan for your life and you need to experience whatever you are going through. May I also say, if God directed our steps to have the heartache then God is with us while we are in the midst of heartache. No, you are not alone when that step comes. God is with you!

Let me say to those who have not taken that step, enjoy the ease of life that you may be in now realizing that there is but one step between you and hardships in life. Before that step is ever taken, enjoy the step of life you are in right now to its fullest. Do not take it for granted, for when that step comes and you step into the hardships of life, you will wish you would have enjoyed life when it was easy.

As you go throughout this day, keep in mind that one misstep and your life will change forever. Ask God to guide your steps even now as you finish reading this. Ask God to keep you from taking the wrong step in life knowing that you are one step from heartache and possibly one step from ruining your life.

The Christian's Greatest Weapon

1 Samuel 23:10-11
"Then said David, O LORD God of Israel, thy servant hath certainly heard that Saul seeketh to come to Keilah, to destroy the city for my sake. Will the men of Keilah deliver me up into his hand? will Saul come down, as thy servant hath heard? O LORD God of Israel, I beseech thee, tell thy servant. And the LORD said, He will come down."

The greatest weapon that a Christian has in this life is the weapon of prayer. In the battle against Saul, you will notice that David did not rely upon man or weapons to keep him safe, he relied upon God. Notice how he asked God what his next move should be. He did not rely upon technology to help him win his battle. He did not rely upon intelligence to tell him what his next move should be. He only relied upon God through prayer to tell him what his next move should be.

Too many times Christians try to rely upon all the wrong devices to make them successful in the Christian life when the greatest tool available to the Christian is prayer. It is through prayer that great victories are won. It is through prayer that a Christian receives the strength to make it in life. It is through prayer that the Christian can dump his worries and cares upon God. It is through prayer that we can conquer great things for God. Prayer is the most valuable tool that a Christian has, and yet, it is the most neglected tool that a Christian possesses.

I want you to notice one other thing about the prayer life of David. In David's prayer life, he was very plain spoken to God when he prayed. Christian, when you pray, just talk to God as you would talk to man. You do not have to be eloquent in your prayer life for your prayers to be heard and answered. It is not the eloquence of prayer that grabs the attention of God; it is the voice of the child of God calling upon Him that grabs His attention. God just wants to hear from you.

I ask you, have you used the greatest weapon in your Christian arsenal today? Have you used the tool of prayer to get wisdom for this day? Have you run to God today to tell Him your needs that must be met? Your only hope in making it through this Christian life is to have a prayer life.

I beg of you, whatever you do, be sure to pray. Have a set time when you daily spend time with God in prayer. When you do pray, be plain spoken to God realizing that He is not impressed by how eloquent you are; He is only concerned with you being you in your prayers to Him.

Weather The Storm

Proverbs 17:14
"The beginning of strife is as when one letteth out water: therefore leave off contention, before it be meddled with."

College sports have always been one of my favorite things to watch. One of the things I like about college sports is the enthusiasm that is involved in the game. When I see the players playing, I see they are playing for the pride of their team and not for the sake of money.

You will notice if you are a fan of college sports that the visiting team in most cases just has to weather the initial emotional front of the other team before they can really get their game plan into effect. If in the start of the game, when the emotions are high, the visiting team can stay within reach of the score, then they have a good chance of being able to win the game. The reason being is eventually the heat of emotion will wear off and once the emotion is gone, then the character of the team must kick in if they are going to win.

This is very much the case with this verse. God was teaching us that the worst part of strife is the very beginning. God uses water that has been held back as an illustration. Once the water is let go, the initial water pressure is stronger, but once the back pressure of the water is let go, then the pressure will subside.

Likewise this is the case with strife. The initial heat of strife is worse at the beginning, then it will let off after it is let go awhile. This is why we must not react at the initial attack of strife. We must weather the storm of the initial attack before deciding how we are going to handle this problem.

This principle must be followed especially in marriages. When married couples have an argument, it is always the start of the argument or the disagreement that is the worst. This is why married couples should never make a decision about their marriage based on what happened during the beginning of an argument or disagreement. God says to leave it alone and move on. You will make many foolish decisions in your marriage that you will regret later on if you base those decisions on what happened at the beginning of an argument or disagreement.

We must apply this principle to all disagreements in life. Whether the disagreement happens at work, church, among friends or with casual acquaintances, never react at the beginning of an argument or disagreement. Always wait for the initial heated feelings to cool down before deciding how you will respond to a disagreement. Many foolish and regretful decisions are made during these times.

So, when strife, arguments and disagreements happen, first of all just be quiet. Then after you are quiet you need to wait until both sides have cooled down. Then you can start deciding on how to handle the situation once cooler heads are presiding. Always remember to weather the initial storm before you make any decisions. If you will remember to weather the storm, then you will find yourself not making foolish decisions.

Uniquely Designed

Psalm 139:14
"I will praise thee; for I am fearfully and wonderfully made: marvellous are thy works; and that my soul knoweth right well."

How would you feel if you specially made something and then the one you made it for made fun of it or didn't like it? This is exactly what we do to God when we make fun of a person's features or when we don't like how God has made us.

A powerful phrase is mentioned in this verse to show us that each and every one of us is uniquely designed of God. That phrase is, *"...I am fearfully and wonderfully made..."* This would mean that everyone in the condition that they are made is made that way on purpose because God uniquely designed for them to be made this way. No matter what we think our physical frailties are, we must understand that was part of God's uniqueness to us.

God made each of us in a separate mold. Some think that they are too skinny and some think they are too fat. Some think that they are too tall and some think they are too short. Some think that their nose is too big and some think it is too small. Some think they don't have enough hair while others don't like the color of their hair. We could go on and on, but each of us, no matter what we don't like about ourselves, was uniquely designed by God.

We may not like some feature about ourselves, but we must understand that God made us this way. We live in a day when the plastic surgeon will change our features when we don't like them. Now don't get me wrong, I know some people have to have a surgery to change features because of health issues. What I am talking about is a society that literally worships the body so much that we are changing the way God made us. What we don't like about ourselves is something

181

that God gave to us to be unique. We must accept this as God's gift to us.

I think of some friends of mine who have a child who is what we would call a "special needs child." We may call this child deformed, but may I say that this child was formed by God. Who are we to say this child is deformed when God is the One Who made this child? Who are doctors and politicians to say that we should kill a child like this in the womb? These children and people are uniquely designed by God for some special purpose. What a blessing these children can be to society if we will not treat them as freaks.

This is why it is so wicked to make fun of people because of some physical feature that was given to them by God. This is why we must be careful about trying to change our features through surgery, because we are *"fearfully and wonderfully made."* This is also the reason we need to learn to accept ourselves the way we are, God made us this way for some special purpose.

Accept what you physically are as a unique design by God. Don't ever wonder and question why God made you the way you are, He has a reason for it and we must find that reason to use for His glory. So whatever it is today that you are constantly trying to cover up because you don't like how you were designed, accept it and realize that God is the One Who designed you this way.

That I May Show Kindness

2 Samuel 9:3
"And the king said, Is there not yet any of the house of Saul, that I may shew the kindness of God unto him? And Ziba said unto the king, Jonathan hath yet a son, which is lame on his feet."

Webster's Dictionary defines *"kindness"* as "good will" or "that which delights in contributing to the happiness of others." In other words, showing kindness to someone is doing something to someone to make them happy.

This is what David did in this passage. David realized that God had blessed him in a great way. David felt he should show kindness to others because of the kindnesses God and others had showed to him. Even though Saul and Jonathan were dead, David wanted to show kindness to them by being kind to someone else. Because of this desire, Mephibosheth was the recipient of David's kindness.

How in today's world we need people to show kindness to someone every day. We live in a society that does not want to show kindness to people because we are out for number one: ourselves. What a tragedy!

I want you to notice something about kindness. Kindness is not about us getting something out of it. The definition itself tells us that kindness is about making someone else happy. There is nothing in the definition of kindness that shows us that we are the recipient of something when we are kind.

This is why most people are not kind. Most people are only going to be kind to someone if they feel they are going to receive something out of it. True kindness is doing good will where you cannot receive anything in return. If you are doing something to receive something back, then this is not kindness.

Every day we ought to look for opportunities to be kind to someone else. Everyday we should find a person to whom we can show good will to simply for the sake of being kind.

I ask you, have you been kind to someone lately? I mean, have you showed good will to someone without expecting anything in return?

Today, and everyday, look for someone to whom you can be kind. Make it your daily goal to show kindness to someone. Show kindness today by letting someone have the last item on sale. Show kindness by letting someone pull out in front of you on the street. Show kindness to someone today and pay for their item at the store. Find someone today whom you can show good will toward who can do nothing in return for you. Just find someone to be kind to today!

Emotional Reigns

2 Samuel 13:30-31
"And it came to pass, while they were in the way, that tidings came to David, saying, Absalom hath slain all the king's sons, and there is not one of them left. Then the king arose, and tare his garments, and lay on the earth; and all his servants stood by with their clothes rent."

The story in this verse is tragic, but it is in the Bible to teach us some very valuable lessons. Here we read how Absalom had waited a long time to get even with his brother Amnon for raping his sister, Tamar. Absalom had a feast for all the sons of David in his house for the purpose of having Amnon killed for his act against Tamar. The Bible states that when Amnon was killed, all the sons of David fled from the house. Word got back to David that Absalom had killed all of his sons. At this word, David rose from the throne and tore his garments to weep for what had seemingly happened to all his sons. We read that a nephew of David came and told him that Amnon was the only one slain. At the hearing of this news, David's heart was comforted.

A very valuable lesson can be learned from this tragic story that will help all of us when tragedy and heartache come our way. Normally, at the first news of tragedy and heartache it sounds very bad. If you rely on the initial reports that you receive concerning tragedy and heartache, it will seem as if the world has ended. If you wait long enough before you react, you will find that tragedy and heartache are never as bad as we first believe. This is why, when tragedy and heartache come, we must learn to wait before we react.

I like to tell people when these times come, put a reign on your emotions so you don't become unstable during the tragedy and heartache. Let me explain!

When tragedy and heartache hit, and the bad reports come in, pull back on your emotional reigns and realize that it is probably not as bad as it originally sounds. Likewise, when you start hearing good reports about the tragedy, don't get too excited because it probably is not quite as good as what you are hearing.

If you are not careful and you respond to the good and bad that you hear about tragedy and heartache, you will find your emotions swinging wildly from good to bad. This is why I say put some reigns on your emotions, and don't get too down from the bad news, and don't get too excited about the good news. Keep yourself on an even keel so you can make proper decisions during these times.

I believe if you will practice this principle, you will keep yourself from becoming an emotional wreck when tragedy and heartache come. Just remember, when tragedy and heartache come, and the reports start flowing in, first of all take a deep breath and wait. Immediately call on God and ask for His wisdom and help during these times. Then, once the dust has settled and you have controlled your emotions, you can help others during their times of tragedy and heartache because you have not lost face during yours due to your emotional swings.

The Sin Of Disloyalty

2 Samuel 17:23
"And when Ahithophel saw that his counsel was not followed, he saddled his ass, and arose, and gat him home to his house, to his city, and put his household in order, and hanged himself, and died, and was buried in the sepulchre of his father."

David, during his reign, had counselors that gave him advice concerning the decisions that he had to make just like the President of the United States has his Cabinet that advises him. One of David's counselors was Ahithophel. When Absalom rebelled against his father, Ahithophel was one of the men who became disloyal to David and followed Absalom. Not only did he follow Absalom, but his disloyalty to David was intensified by giving counsel to Absalom on how to destroy David.

In the verse above, we see where disloyalty led Ahithophel. It led him to shame and eventually to so much shame that he committed suicide. What a sad ending to such a fruitful mind. Yet, this is where disloyalty always leads a person. O, it might not lead them to suicide, but it will lead them on a path of disenchantment and self-worthlessness.

Disloyalty is a terrible sin in that it not only is a disobedience to authority, but it is also a breaking of your word to authority. All followers must learn that disloyalty cannot be tolerated. Disloyalty will hurt a cause or an organization to the point that it may never recover once it has started. It is like a disease that will spread and will not only destroy you, but also the innocent in that organization who are not disloyal.

Disloyalty is talking against authority behind their back. Disloyalty is a plant manager or supervisor who talks negatively about the company to other employees. Disloyalty is staff members talking to others in the congregation about how they disagree with the authority. How wicked and sinful is this sin!

Now if you are one who has a disagreement with an authority, there are two proper moves you can make. First, go and talk to the authority in an undemanding way about your disagreements or concerns. Do not go in there demanding or with an attitude for it will get you nowhere. But let me advise those in positions of authority, you had better listen to someone who comes in to you this way and do not just brush them off. If you don't listen, you are setting the seed for disloyalty in their hearts. They want to know why, so give them your answer. Don't just shove them aside or give them an answer and then not follow through.

Second, if you can't agree with the explanation of authority and cannot live with what they are going to do without causing problems, then you must quietly leave. Leave in such a manner that everyone else would not know why you have left.

Each of us must be careful that we are not disloyal to those with whom we work. If you are being disloyal, then you need to get your heart and attitude right with God and with your authority. Whatever you do, do not become disloyal for disloyalty will kill you spiritually and cause you not to enjoy life.

Recipe For Victory

2 Samuel 23:10
"He arose, and smote the Philistines until his hand was weary, and his hand clave unto the sword: and the LORD wrought a great victory that day; and the people returned after him only to spoil."

I love it when God gives us recipes to accomplish great tasks for Him. We have one of those recipes in this verse.

David was now at the end of his life. As his life is coming to a close, David puts together a list of men whom he called his mighty men. In this list, there were three men whom David called his three mightiest men. One of the three was Eleazar the son of Dodo. David tells us the thing that made Eleazar a mighty man was that he went to war against the Philistine army all by himself. David then makes the statement that when his hand became weary in the battle he clave unto the sword that was in his hand until the battle was over. Eleazar determined that though he was tired, the one thing he would not let go of was the sword. I see a recipe for victory in this story.

First, you cannot run from the battle. Notice that others *"were gone away"* while he stayed. You will never have victory in any area of life if you constantly run from battles. Sometime in your life you must decide that running from battles is not the answer. The reason why some people never have victory in life is because they run when the battles come. They have never had victory because they have never given themselves a chance to have victory. If you are going to have victory in your life, you must not run when battles come your way. I am saying, STOP running away from your battles and face them!

Second, the Bible says *"He arose."* Not only must you not run from the battle, but you must also do something about the battle. The sword is not going to fight by itself. You will

189

never have victory in life by talking about what needs to get done. Whatever it is, you must rise up and fight the battle that you face. Victories are won because someone decided they must fight the battle. I am saying, whatever dream or desire you have for your life you must rise up and go after that desire or dream no matter how hard it may get. You will not have victory in that area without rising up.

Third, when weary you must keep on going. Even though Eleazar was weary, he did not stop fighting. When you get tired of the battle you must keep on fighting. When you get tired of standing for right, you must continue to stand for right. When you get tired of trying to make your marriage successful, you must continue to fight to make your marriage successful. When you get tired of trying to make your business successful, you must continue to fight to make it successful. Weariness is not a good enough excuse to quit. Those who are successful in life and experience victory continue on though weary.

Finally, if you want victory you must cleave to the sword. In the Bible, God uses the sword as a symbol for the Bible. In other words, if you want victory in any area of life, you must cleave to the Bible. You will never have victory over sin without the Bible. You will never have victory in any pursuit or area of life without the Bible. The Bible is the tool a Christian must use if they want victory. That means if you want victory, you must read It and live according to what It says.

So whatever battle you face today, take this recipe and apply it realizing that if it worked for Eleazar it will work for you. If you will just apply it, I know you can do it!

A Common Mistake Of Leadership

1 Kings 2:42-43
"And the king sent and called for Shimei, and said unto him, Did I not make thee to swear by the LORD, and protested unto thee, saying, Know for a certain, on the day thou goest out, and walkest abroad any whither, that thou shalt surely die? and thou saidst unto me, The word that I have heard is good. Why then hast thou not kept the oath of the LORD, and the commandment that I have charged thee with?"

One mistake that leadership makes quite often is to let the established rules be broken.

Solomon made a decree to Shimei that if he left the city of Jerusalem he would die. Now the truth is, Shimei's reason for having to leave the city may have seemed like a legitimate reason, but the problem was if he let him go for this reason, then he would have to let him go for another legitimate reason. The rules were established by both sides and that meant that they both must follow the rules. If not, then leadership would have been weakened and eventually Solomon would have lost his kingdom to a disloyal person.

Leadership must be careful about letting people who break the rules slide by. Rules are there for a purpose and that purpose is they are to be kept and not broken. What happens many times is leadership thinks it is just a small rule and because of this, they let them go. On top of this, many times leadership does not want to be confrontational toward a person who is breaking a rule. If leadership wants to establish its authority, then leadership must adhere to the established rules. If not, then leadership will lose their authority.

I ask you, as a parent, are you letting your children get away with breaking the rules in the home? It does not matter how insignificant it is, if you as a parent are going to establish your leadership in the home, then you must as a leader enforce those rules. Likewise this question could be asked of the job supervisor, plant manager, school teacher, school principal, church leadership and even city officials and civil servants. Leadership is only as strong as their enforcement of the established rules.

Let's be careful about letting people get by with breaking even the smallest of rules. If the rules are broken, then there must be consequences. If we don't enforce the rules, then there is no purpose for those rules to be in the books. Leadership will only be established to the degree that it enforces the rules that they are supposed to uphold. Until you as a leader do this, you will find yourself having problems with the people following you.

A Make-Believe World

1 Kings 2:15
"And he said, Thou knowest that the kingdom was mine, and that all Israel set their faces on me, that I should reign: howbeit the kingdom is turned about, and is become my brother's: for it was his from the LORD."

Adonijah had the same problem that many people seem to have today. His problem was that he refused to live in reality but instead chose to live in a make believe world.

In the verse above, Adonijah came to the mother of Solomon and asked her for the young lady that nursed King David when he was old. As Adonijah gives his request to Bathsheba, the mother of Solomon, he makes the statement that the kingdom was his. Now this was not a true statement. In his mind, the kingdom was his, but in reality the kingdom had never officially been handed over to him. The kingdom never was his and was never going to be his. Adonijah's problem was he chose to live in a make-believe world hoping that it would eventually become reality. The reality was, his make-believe world was only holding him back from pursuing things in his life that would make him a better man.

Herein lays the problem with most people. They imagine something in their minds and want to live in this imagination which is nothing but make believe. This is why God says to cast down imaginations in 2 Corinthians 10:5.

For instance, I have run across many people who continue to try and live in the past when in all reality the past is over and all they are doing is continuing to live in a make-believe world. Your past is done, and now you must move on to the present which is reality. There are some who live in a make-believe world of wrong relationships. This is where the world of pornography is so deceitful. They get people to live in make-believe world's trying to fulfill a fantasy which is not real. By doing this, they hurt those who are in the real world they live in; the world of their marriage and their home. There are also others who live in a make-believe world of finances thinking that they have more money than they truly have. They try to impress people with what they have by buying cars, houses and possessions that are well above their financial status. By doing this, they get themselves into huge debt. These people simply are refusing to live in a world of reality, and that reality is they just don't have the money that they try to portray to everyone else. Most of the problems we face in life are because we refuse to live in the world of reality and instead choose to live in a make believe world.

I ask you, are you living in a make-believe world? Are you living in a fantasy and refuse to live in the reality of the world in which you live? Until you stop living in a make-believe world, you will continue to hurt those in the real world that you live in. While you live in a make-believe world in your mind, you are holding yourself back from the world of reality. Whether this world is your home, your marriage, your job, your finances or even your age, whatever it is, you will never see these areas flourish until you leave your make-believe world.

Don't be like Adonijah who hurt himself by living in his little make-believe world. Realize make believe is only that, it is make believe. Live in the real world by facing reality and you will further yourself in life.

What Are Your Motives And Intentions?

1 Kings 8:18
"And the LORD said unto David my father, Whereas it was in thine heart to build an house unto my name, thou didst well that it was in thine heart."

Of all the things that God chose to tell us about David, it was the heart of David that God mentions over and over again. In fact, in this verse it says that God was pleased that it was in David's heart to build a temple for God. God was more pleased that David wanted and intended to do something for Him than He was by the action of trying to actually build the temple.

The phrase, *"...thou didst well that it was in thine heart"* is talking about the motives and intentions of the heart of David. God was pleased that David had the right motives and the right intentions. The intentions of David's heart were to do right. The motives of his heart were to do right. He was not doing things to impress others; he was doing things because it was in his heart to do them. It mattered not to David whether anyone else wanted to do this; he wanted to do right because it was the motive and intentions of his heart.

Everyone should learn from this that God is more interested in your motives than He is with anything else. Yes, God wants us to have the right actions, but what God desires more is right within our hearts. It is the motives of the heart that will eventually come out. This is why God says in Proverbs 23:7, *"For as he thinketh in his heart, so is he."* You will eventually become whatever the intentions and motives are in your heart.

I ask you, what are the motives of your heart? What are the intentions behind what you do? Are the intentions and motives of your heart to hold some great position in society or in the church? Do you do everything so that you can one day hold some "great position" that man will notice? Are the intentions and motives of your heart to have wealth or fame? Ask yourself this question, "Why is it that I do what I am doing?" Your answer to this question will show the intentions and motives of your heart.

Now the question is this, what was your answer? If your answer was about anything else other than to bring glory to God, then your intentions and motives are wrong. The Bible states in 1 Corinthians 10:31 that all that we do in life should bring glory to God. If our motives and intentions are not to bring glory to God, then we need to change our motives and intentions. When our motives and intentions are to bring glory to God, then God will be pleased with that which is in our hearts.

Would God say about you, *"thou didst well that it was in thine heart."* When God looks at your motives and intentions, is He pleased? If not, then change the motives and intentions of your heart to only do that which will bring glory to God. If your motives or intentions are for your glory, then stop what you're doing. Only do that for which the motives and intentions of your heart are right.

Leadership's Classic Mistake

1 King 12:13-15
"And the king answered the people roughly, and forsook the old men's counsel that they gave him; And spake to them after the counsel of the young men, saying, My father made your yoke heavy, and I will add to your yoke: my father also chastised you with whips, but I will chastise you with scorpions. Wherefore the king hearkened not unto the people; for the cause was from the LORD, that he might perform his saying, which the LORD spake by Ahijah the Shilonite unto Jeroboam the son of Nebat."

In this story, Rehoboam made one of the biggest mistakes that leadership can ever make. This mistake is thinking that their place of position is for the people to serve them. This is not the purpose of leadership. Leadership is in place to serve the people and to meet the needs of the people.

When leadership starts thinking that people are to serve them, then leadership will begin to fall. Any great leader who lives on in history as a great leader is a person who used their position to help people.

Herein is the difference between a dictator and a leader. A dictator will use his position to meet his needs and expects people to serve him because of his position. By the way, a dictator shows his poor ability to lead, for he cannot get anyone to follow him as he tries to lead without force or fear of force. A leader uses his position to serve the needs of the people he serves. Being a leader is much harder than being a dictator in the fact that by being a leader the followers have a choice to follow, and yet, the leader is still capable of getting them to follow him without force or fear of force. Rehoboam never learned this principle, and apparently neither did the young men who counseled him. Each leader needs to learn this great principle.

I am talking to the parents who are leaders in your home. Your purpose as a parent is not to use your children to serve you. Your purpose as their leader is to teach them what is the right way in life. Yes, as the leader in the home you may require your children to fulfill certain duties. These duties are not to be done so that you won't have to do them, but they are to be done to teach them how to become a better person in society. This is the case with any level of leadership. All leadership positions are there for the sole purpose to serve those they lead.

Any leader who must use fear to get their followers to continue to follow them is a poor leader. If you want people to follow you, then convince them that you are not out to get them to serve you. Instead, convince them that you are out to meet their needs, and you will be pleasantly surprised how willingly they will follow you.

I ask every leader who reads this, how are your leadership skills? Do people follow you because you serve them, or do they follow you out of fear of what you will do to them if they don't follow you? Let every leader realize the purpose of your position is to serve those you lead. When you fulfill that purpose, then those you lead will want to follow you for they will know that you have their best interest at heart.

Some Good Thing

1 Kings 14:12-13
"Arise thou therefore, get thee to thine own house: and when thy feet enter into the city, the child shall die. And all Israel shall mourn for him, and bury him: for he only of Jeroboam shall come to the grave, because in him there is found some good thing toward the LORD God of Israel in the house of Jeroboam."

The death of a child may be one of the hardest things for people. Not only is it a hard thing for people to understand, but it is also hard to explain to parents why God took their child at such an early age. We know according to the Bible that all things work together for good, but in the midst of heartache it is certainly hard to find any good.

In this verse, we see the man of God advising the wicked king's wife that their child was going to die. There is an interesting statement in this verse that tells us why the child was going to die. The Bible says that God was going to take the child early in his life *"...because in him there is found some good thing toward the LORD God of Israel in the house of Jeroboam."* Did you see why God was taking the child? It was because in the child was something good that God found and He wanted to save the child from the heartache that was going to come because of his dad's sin. Yes, there was a purpose behind the death of that child. The purpose was God was having mercy on the child. Now I certainly don't have all the answers to life, but I do know that in this verse, we can see a few reasons why God takes children to Heaven early.

First, we see that God takes them to Heaven to spare them from the heartache of the impending judgment that God will send upon a parent. Because I have dealt with this one first, please do not take this personally if you have lost a child. There are times when God is trying to wake a parent up and get their attention through the death of their child. Not only is God trying to wake the parent up, but God is showing mercy to that child so they will not have to go through the punishment caused by their parents' sins.

The second reason God takes a child early is because God is sparing that child from the heartache that he would face in life if he were to live. The one thing none of us can do is see the future. Only God can do this. Sometimes in God's mercy, God takes a child home because He knows what heartache they would face in their life if they were to live. Not heartache because of their parents sins, but heartache because of the world they would live in or heartache because of some physical ailment that would come their way. Not all heartache comes because of sin. So God, in His mercy, spares that child from some impending heartache that they would face if they were to live.

Then we see a third reason in this verse. Notice again that the Bible says that there was *"found some good thing"* in this child. I believe the third reason God takes a child early is because God found some good thing in that child that He thinks would make Heaven a better place. What a comforting thought that God would take our child because He felt our child would make Heaven such a better place. I know to those who have lost a child this does not take the pain away, but it can certainly ease the pain knowing that the ministry God had for your child is in Heaven. Yes, God may have allowed your child to go to Heaven early simply because He had a ministry for them there.

Again, I do not imply that I know why God takes a child early and certainly this devotional does not include all the reasons. I do believe that we find some reasons in this verse why God would take a child early. If you are one of those parents whose child God chose to take to Heaven, please look at these three reasons I have given and take comfort in knowing that God had your child's best interest at heart when He made this decision. If you could see what they are doing now in Heaven, you most certainly would agree with God's decision even though it will still hurt you. You can take comfort in knowing this; your child is awaiting your arrival in Heaven some day. Be ready to meet your child by making sure you are right with God and by being sure you are saved.

God's Prescription For Depression

1 Kings 19:15-16
"And the LORD said unto him, Go, return on thy way to the wilderness of Damascus: and when thou comest, anoint Hazael to be king over Syria: And Jehu the son of Nimshi shalt thou anoint to be king over Israel: and Elisha the son of Shaphat of Abelmeholah shalt thou anoint to be prophet in thy room."

I know this may seem a little petty, but I am encouraged when I see in the Bible the great heroes whom we look up to, have the same problems in life that many of us face daily.

This was the case with Elijah. Elijah was in a serious state of depression. Yes, the great prophet of God was depressed to the point where he wanted to take his life. Isn't it interesting that men of God have the same problems that everybody else has? The reason Elijah was in this state of depression is because he had worn himself out to the point that he physically had no power over his own flesh to fight the depression that came his way. God stepped into the life of Elijah and gave him a recipe to get himself out of his depression. Let me show you what worked for Elijah, and then, counsel you to take these same steps when you come to a point in your life when you are depressed this will help you get yourself out of your depression.

Let me first say, I know that some depression is caused by physical ailments and a doctor can help. If your health is not right, it is sure hard to fight off depression.

Let us look at the prescription that God gave for the state of depression that Elijah was in. First, God prescribed Elijah to get some rest. Before God could help Elijah, He knew one of the main reasons the prophet was in this state of mind was because of a lack of rest. If you are the type of person who runs yourself into the ground by working tirelessly, then I would advise you to make sure you get plenty of rest. When you are tired, you let your mind wander a bit into the hard things of life that have come your way which can send you into a state of depression. Be sure if you are one of these types of people, to get some rest so your mind and body can be renewed.

Secondly, we see God telling Elijah to *"Go."* After getting the rest he needed, God knew Elijah wasn't doing anybody any good by sitting under a juniper tree feeling sorry for himself. Many times the best prescription for people who are depressed is to just get up and get busy doing something. Far too many times, people who are depressed are people who sit around feeling sorry for themselves. Now I know this is not popular, but this is the truth. If you have ever been around people who are depressed, you will notice they dwell on themselves all the time. Everything is about them. Well let me be blunt with you, everything is not about you. There is more to this life and in this world than you.

Thirdly, we see God didn't just want him to get up and go, but God wanted him to go and start pouring his life into others. Yes, the best prescription for depression is to get your mind off of yourself by going and helping others. You will find when you go out and start helping others that you get your mind off of yourself and your problems. This will help you immensely when you are feeling sorry for yourself.

Now, not everybody lives in a constant state of depression, but everybody will fight getting depressed at some time in their life. When you start fighting depression, remember this devotional and apply it so that you can quickly recover. In recovering quickly, you will find yourself able to accomplish more things in life. So, do as God told the prophet and go and invest your life into the lives of others. This not only will get you out of a state of depression, but it will also keep you from entering a state of depression.

Handling Disagreements With God's Men

2 Kings 1:15
"And the angel of the LORD said unto Elijah, Go down with him: be not afraid of him. And he arose, and went down with him unto the king."

You will notice a stark difference between the last captain of fifty from the first two captains of fifty. The first two captains were very demanding of the man of God while the last captain was humble in his dealings with the man of God.

There is a principle that God is teaching in this story and I believe that principle is: there is a right way and a wrong way to approach the man of God when you have a disagreement with him. Notice the first two captains were demanding, and God had them killed. Why is that? Because God does not take kindly to people who are demanding of the man of God. There is only One Who can be demanding of men of God and that is God.

When a person has a disagreement with the man of God they should never come to him in a demanding way. I believe what we must understand is even though the man of God is just a man, it is his position that demands respect. We would not go into God's physical presence demanding of Him and telling Him what to do. No, we would come in trembling with fear and would be very respectful towards God. This is where the third captain differed from the first two captains. When he came into the presence of the man of God he was not demanding, but humble.

When you have a disagreement with a man of God you should never come to him with a demanding spirit, for God does not take kindly to this. I also believe a man of God should not deal with a person who comes in with a demanding spirit, for his position demands that he make sure people address him properly.

I am reminded of a story during the American Revolution where the enemy sent a letter to George Washington that addressed him as Mr. and not as General. The men that met these messengers would not allow them to go to General Washington at his command because they were not addressing him properly. It was not that he thought he was something, he thought the position he held deserved respect. Likewise men of God should treat their position with respect and those who have disagreements with men of God should still treat them with respect.

There is nothing wrong with having disagreements with the man of God. There is something wrong with being demanding toward the man of God. Let us all be careful how we approach the man of God when we have disagreements with him. Let us approach him with respect, without demands, honoring the position he holds.

Ho Hum Christianity

2 Kings 13:18-19
"And he said, Take the arrows. And he took them. And he said unto the king of Israel, Smite upon the ground. And he smote thrice, and stayed. And the man of God was wroth with him, and said, Thou shouldest have smitten five or six times; then hadst thou smitten Syria till thou hadst consumed it: whereas now thou shalt smite Syria but thrice."

In the story that we read in this passage of Scripture, Israel was under great oppression from the king of Syria. Elisha had fallen sick and Joash, the king of Israel, had come to pay his last respects to the dying man of God. Apparently these two had a good working relationship with each other, and Joash was sorrowful over the fact that the man of God was going to die. Elisha, in his last act before he died, commanded Joash to take and shoot an arrow. Joash did just this! Elisha told Joash that this arrow which he shot represented that God was going to deliver Israel from Syria. Then Elisha told Joash to smite the arrows upon the ground. Joash took the arrows and he only smote the ground three times. Elisha was upset because Joash should have been so vigorous in wanting God to destroy the Syrians that he should have smitten the ground many more times.

Yet I see the same problem in most people today when it comes to God's work and that is, they are so passive about the work of the LORD. How sad that Christians are passive about doing the greatest work in all the world. What a nation needs and what our churches need are people who are zealous for God and want God to do something great instead of being ho hum about God's work.

I ask you, are you passive about the preaching of the Word of God? Do you just sit there in your seat at church with no emotion when God's Word is being preached? Do you respond during the invitation time, or do you stand in your seat anxiously waiting for the services to end? Are you passive about God's work being accomplished? Are you going to church only to fulfill your religious obligation? Is serving God only a portion of your life, or are you consumed with serving God?

What God wants is a people consumed with service to Him. This was the problem with Joash; he was not as consumed with God's work as Elisha was.

If every Christian would check their heart, and renew their fire of revival and become consumed and passionate again about God's work, we would most certainly see circumstances change in our country. If only we could walk into churches again and see people with an excitement about God's work, I believe we would then see churches begin to grow again. This is what will change cities, counties, states and countries; a people passionate about God's work.

Today, why don't you become a person who is passionate and zealous for the work of the LORD. Let it consume you and be a part of all your being. Don't be a Joash, be an Elisha!

My Fear For My Nation

2 Kings 17:18
"Therefore the LORD was very angry with Israel, and removed them out of his sight: there was none left but the tribe of Judah only."

When I read this chapter, my heart is touched and moved as I think of the United States, my nation. I see great similarities between the nation of Israel and the United States when it comes to God's blessings.

I do not believe anyone can deny that God has blessed America in a great way. When I read of her history and study the founding of America, there is no doubt that God, Jehovah God, was a part in its founding. But, when I read this chapter and look at the sins of Israel, I am again reminded of America and what she is like today.

In this chapter God goes through a list of sins that Israel had committed that brought God's wrath upon them. What were these sins? Some of these sins included: idolatry, lack of standards, a politically correct society, rejection of God's Word, refusing to listen to the preachers of their day, living for the vanities of the world and the sacrificing their children for the sake of their gods. What a terrible list of sins that Israel had committed. Yet, America has committed the exact same sins that are listed in this chapter.

Let us look at the end of this lifestyle. The end was the judgment of God upon Israel. The end was God removing Israel out of His sight for several years and lowering Israel to serve other nations who used to serve them. Yes, if we are not careful, God can do the same to America. America is not above the judgment of God and let us not feel that we are. God will judge America for these sins just like He judged Israel for them.

What is the answer? The answer is always within the Christians who live in America. The answer is you! My fear for my nation is if we do not start changing the way we live then one day we will face the exact same end that Israel faced in this passage of Scripture. If the people of our nation do not wake up and change their ways, then God has no choice but to bring His judgment upon this land. Let's be honest with each other. To those who are getting upset with me while you are reading this, could you honestly say that America is what she ought to be? Can you honestly tell me there is a difference between America and what Israel was in those days? You could not! The only hope and the only answer is God's people.

God has always left it up to His people to change their ways before He would hold back His judgment upon their nation. This means, if you and I change the way we live and do what is right, then we can stay the judgment of God upon our nation. It all starts with one person doing right. If we all wait for everyone else to do right, then no one will end up doing right.

Today, as you go throughout your day, remember to do right. Remember that by you doing right, you might influence others to do right. If each of us will do right ourselves, then I truly believe that we can change our nation. Let us not be guilty of becoming like the nation of Israel who forgot the God that blessed her and made her. Let each of us live right regardless if anyone else does right. Let us not be the ones who are guilty of bringing God's judgment upon our land because we are the ones who commit the sins that we read about in this chapter.

And He Did

2 Kings 20:8
"And Hezekiah said unto Isaiah, What shall be the sign that the LORD will heal me, and that I shall go up into the house of the LORD the third day?"

An age old problem is seen in this verse in the life of Hezekiah. Hezekiah is sick and the Prophet Isaiah came to tell him that he was going to die. As Hezekiah heard he was going to die, instead of griping to people or whining about his sickness, he went to the source that could help him; God. God heard the prayer of Hezekiah and sent the Prophet Isaiah back to the king to tell him that God heard his prayer and that He was going to heal Hezekiah. What a time of rejoicing this should have been. What a time of praising God for Hezekiah. Instead we see a problem that most people face in that Hezekiah didn't believe God's Word and wanted a sign from God that this was really going to happen. Hezekiah, where is your faith? Why do you need a sign from God when you have God's Word on it? God's Word should have been enough.

Yet this happens to God's people over and over again. There are people who do not have the faith to trust God's Word and constantly need a sign from God. I ask you, has God's Word ever failed? God said that He would deliver Israel from Egypt, and He did. God said He would bring the Israelites into the Promised Land, and He did. God said that He would send a Saviour for the world, and He did. God said that Jesus would rise again from the dead, and He did. God said that He would save us from our sins if we would call on Him and ask Him to save us, and He has. We could go on and on and on in the list of what God said He would do, and He has.

Let me remind everyone who reads this, if God says He is going to do something, you don't need a sign from Him that He is going to do it. If God says, if you put Him first that He will bless you, then He will. If God says, He will supply your needs, then He will. If God says, He will never leave or forsake you, then He will always be with you. If God says, He will bless you if you do right, then He will. If God says that something is going to happen, then IT WILL!

O Christian, today as you go throughout the day, take God's Word and bank on it. Though things may be unstable in society, let me assure you God can and will come through on His Word just like He says He will. Stop living by sight and live by faith. Put your trust in His Word and realize that He will come through if He says He will.

What is it that you doubt right now? If you will simply do what God has told you to do, then you can rest assured based on the Word of God that He will do what He says He is going to do.

A Sermon From The Grave

2 Kings 23:17
"Then he said, What title is that that I see? And the men of the city told him, It is the sepulchre of the man of God, which came from Judah, and proclaimed these things that thou hast done against the altar of Bethel."

As I write this devotional, it is near the anniversary of my mother's homegoing. I was reminded a bit of her as I read this verse about Josiah going through the cemetery removing all the sepulchers of the prophets of Baal. When they came to this one sepulcher, the Bible says they did not destroy it because inside of it were the bones of the prophet of God that testified of the works of Josiah. When Josiah found out that it was the bones of this prophet of God, he told them to leave those bones alone. I believe he wanted that sepulcher to be a remembrance of the preaching of this great prophet.

As I read this, my thought was, if you were to die today, of what would your graveside marker remind others? You see, I thought of my mother during these past few days and remembered with fondness the great example that she was to me in her lifetime. What example have you been to others? What sermon would your graveside preach to others? It will preach some sermon, but will it be the sermon you wanted it to preach? Would your graveside preach a sermon about a life lived for God and a life of being good to others? Or would your graveside be a reminder of a wasted life because of all the bad that you have done? It will remind people of one or the other.

One other thought comes to mind as I think of this. Have you done anything that would cause people to remember anything about you? Let's face it, some people do nothing in life that would cause anyone to remember anything about them when they die. These people who do nothing are just forgotten. How sad this is! Every one of us ought to desire to leave some good work behind in our life. Every one of us ought to live a life so that when we are gone others will have good memories about what we have done.

I ask you again, if you died today, would your graveside marker preach a sermon of a good life lived to inspire others to do right? Or, would your graveside marker preach a sermon that warns of the dangers of living a wicked life? Let all of us today and everyday live our lives in such a way that we have something good to leave behind. Let us make sure that our days are not wasted doing nothing. Let us live them doing good so we will leave behind a good testimony.

More Honourable

1 Chronicles 4:9
"And Jabez was more honourable than his brethren: and his mother called his name Jabez, saying, Because I bare him with sorrow."

We find in the midst of the genealogies of the Chronicles a man by the name of Jabez. We do not know much about his life other than these two verses in chapter 4. The one thing we know about him is that he was born in sorrow. I don't know what the sorrow was that his mother was going through, but notice even in the midst of sorrow his mother had a child who could bring her joy.

The one thing I want you to notice about Jabez is that the Bible states he was *"more honourable"* than his brethren. You see, it matters not what others are doing, you can always be more honorable than them. Maybe society at his time was living in a wrong manner, but he decided to be more honorable than them by doing right. Maybe his brethren treated him wrong because of the conditions of his birth, but he was more honorable than them by treating them right.

We must learn that it does not matter what everyone else does, it only matters what we do. It does not matter how others treat us, we must be more honorable and treat them right. It does not matter how your spouse treats you, you must be more honorable and treat them right. It does not matter how a coworker, a fellow student at your school or how any other person treats you, you must be more honorable and do what is right. Just because another person does you wrong, you must learn not to react to their actions but become more honorable and do right. This is what Jabez did in his life.

Yet there is one other thought that we can learn from this verse. The word *"honourable"* means "to be heavy" or "weighty." In other words, sometimes it will not be easy to be more honorable than other people. Sometimes it is a heavy thing to be more honorable than others. No matter how heavy or how hard it may be to be honorable, we as Christians must be more honorable than others, and do what is right though they may not do right.

As you go through your day, remember to be more honorable than others. I am not talking about thinking or acting like you are better, I am talking about just doing better. Remember, it may be hard to be more honorable than another person, but let us be a people who are more honorable than others. Let us be a people who when others do us wrong are more honorable because we do right to them no matter how they treat us.

Preparing For Leadership

1 Chronicles 12:39
"And there they were with David three days, eating and drinking: for their brethren had prepared for them."

In the making of great leadership, it takes people who prepare others to follow in order for that leader to become great.

At the time when the brethren in this verse were preparing others in Israel to follow David, they did not know that David would become the greatest king of Israel. They also did not know at this time that he would become a man after God's own heart. All they knew is that he was anointed and called of God to become the king of Israel. So, because David was the anointed of God, they helped prepare everyone in Israel to follow him. Without them preparing others to follow David, we may never have had King David, the greatest king of Israel.

All throughout history we have heard and read of great leaders. We love to buy books on leadership and read them to learn what made these men the great leaders they were. Yet, I believe in every book on leadership, one key element that helped these men to become the great leaders that they were is missing. That element was that there were a people who were willing to follow those leaders. Without the followers following these leaders, they would have never become the great leaders that they were.

Likewise, there is someone who you are under right now. Your leader can only become a great leader if you and everyone else with you will follow them. This is why there must be some under every leader who prepares others to follow them. There must be some who, behind the scenes, help others to get behind the leadership. Leaders will never become great leaders without the type of people who help prepare others to follow.

Wouldn't it be sad if the leader you have right now could become a great leader but they will never be able to show their leadership abilities because no one under them is preparing others to follow them? Without someone preparing others to follow the leader, the leader will never reach their potential. It is always easy to criticize leadership, but there must be people who prepare others to follow a leader in order for that leader to become great.

Why don't you become that person for your leader? Why not decide to help your leader reach their potential by helping to prepare others to follow them. Whether this leader is your pastor, your parents, your boss, your community leader or whoever it may be, they need you to help prepare others to follow.

The Wisdom Of God

1 Chronicles 14:13-14
"And the Philistines yet again spread themselves abroad in the valley. Therefore David enquired again of God; and God said unto him, Go not up after them; turn away from them, and come upon them over against the mulberry trees."

I believe in this verse we see one of the reasons why David was such a successful king. As David went to war against the Philistines, in verse 10 of this chapter, we see David asked God whether or not he should go up against them. God responded by telling David to go ahead and go to war against them. When we come to this verse, again we see David asked God whether or not he should go up against the Philistines. God responded by telling him to go up a different way than he went originally. The secret to all of this was David, every time he was faced with a decision, asked God for His wisdom on what he should do. David realized that the wisdom of God was greater than the wisdom of man. He also realized that no matter what he did, he always needed God's wisdom.

This principle that David lived by will most certainly help everyone who reads this devotional. It doesn't matter what you are faced with in life, if you want to do the right thing and be successful in what you are doing you need the wisdom of God. There is no task so small that you don't need God's wisdom. It is getting the wisdom of God that will guide you to success in everything you do.

Too many times we try to do things alone and then find ourselves in a mess because we didn't get God's wisdom. You need the wisdom of God in everything you do far more than you need a college education.

In everything you do, you should ask God for His wisdom to know what to do. Every parent should ask God for His wisdom on how to help rear their children. Every businessman should ask God for His wisdom before stepping out on a business venture. Every person, no matter what the task, should ask God for His wisdom on what, and how, they should do what they are about to do.

Today, as you go throughout the day, before you type a letter, drive your car, make a meal, start your job or whatever you must do, simply ask God in a small prayer for His wisdom to do what you need to do. Then before each task that you are faced with today and every day, no matter how small it may seem, just say to God in a small prayer, "God, please give me Your wisdom to do this task that I am about to do." You will find things will become much easier to do when you get the wisdom of God for the task that you are faced with in life. Just be sure to not do the task alone in your wisdom, get the wisdom of God and life will become much easier.

The Responsibility Of Thanks And Praise

1 Chronicles 23:30
"And to stand every morning to thank and praise the LORD, and likewise at even;"

In the temple of the LORD, God divided the duties of the Levites and the priests. The Levites were to be helpers to the priests in accomplishing the duties of the temple. In fact, in verse 28 God says their job was to *"wait on the sons of Aaron for the service of the house of the LORD."* The word *"wait"* means "to serve" like a waiter or waitress would serve their patrons in a restaurant. One of the ways they were to serve is seen in verse 30 where it says that every morning and evening they were to stand and thank and praise the LORD. Yes, this was a responsibility and not a choice. Why would God give them this responsibility? Because God wanted their praise and thanks for the good things He has done for them.

I believe every Christian, every morning and every night, should thank and praise God for what He has done for them. Every morning we should thank the LORD for what He did for us the day before. Every morning we should praise the LORD for His goodness and protection over us throughout the previous day and throughout the night. Every night we should stop and thank and praise the LORD for how He helped us throughout the day and for His goodness to us. I am saying this is not a choice; it is our responsibility to praise and thank the LORD for what He has done for us.

Here is what I find among most of God's people. Instead of praising and thanking Him for what He has done, we complain and gripe about what we think He has not done. I ask you, are you one of those who complain or gripe about what you think God has not done for you, or are you one of those who thanks and praises the LORD for what He has done? It takes character to thank and praise the LORD daily for His goodness to us. It is selfish to gripe about what He has not done. Now which one do you find yourself doing?

Be sure to purposely, every morning and night, set a few minutes aside to thank God for what He has done for you the previous day, and praise Him for His power and goodness towards you. I find the best time for me to do this is first thing in the morning, before I read my Bible, and the last thing at night before I go to bed.

Be a person who God can count on to hear thanks and praise from every morning and every evening.

Right Perspective Concerning Money

1 Chronicles 29:16
"O LORD our God, all this store that we have prepared to build thee an house for thine holy name cometh of thine hand, and is all thine own."

One of the mistakes we make as Christians is thinking that when we give to God we are giving of our own possessions or belongings. We learn from this verse that all we give to God is not ours because it all belongs to God. Think with me, God gives to us, and then when we give back to God. In reality, we are giving Him what is already His. This doesn't seem like much of a gift, but God is pleased when we give to Him. There are two truths that we learn from this verse that I believe will be very helpful in how we think concerning giving.

First of all, everything we get comes from God. This is where many people make a mistake. When a person makes a lot of money, many times they will feel that they have made this money, so it is theirs. Quite the opposite is true! We all must learn that whatever we own is not really ours but God's. If we will learn this principle, this will solve all of our problems with pride.

We live in a day when we talk all the time about the different classes of people. We have the poor and middle class, and then we have what society calls the rich. Let me remind everyone, that in all reality, all of us are the same in God's eyes. God does not think more of us because we have more money or less of us because we are poor. Everything we own is really God's in the first place. If we will learn this, we will see that we should not think better or worse of people because of the amount of money they possess or don't possess.

Secondly, when we give to God let us not think that we are doing something that makes us a great Christian. All that we give to God is His in the first place. Sometimes, if we are not careful, we will think that we are some super Christian because we gave more than someone else. Ok, so you gave more, you only gave back to God what was His in the first place. Now don't get me wrong, I believe in giving to God and even giving sacrificially when the situation demands it. But what we must learn is, giving to God is only giving back to Him what already belongs to Him.

This is why giving should not be a grievous thing to do. It is His in the first place, so why do we think we can hold back from God what is rightfully His? If God asks us to give Him His possessions back, it should not be a hard thing to do for they are already His.

This is why God says we have robbed Him when we don't pay our tithes. The money is His and when we won't give it back we have literally robbed Him.

Let us keep this thought in our minds when it comes to giving. Let us remember that everything we have belongs to God, and that when we are giving to God we are only giving back to Him that which is rightfully His. These truths will help us to keep our money, possessions and giving in the right perspective.

Products Available from Domelle Ministries

Preaching CD Albums

- Staying on Top Side
- Lighting Your Own Fire
- Caution, Hot Preaching Ahead
- Sermons for Struggling Christians
- Relationships with God and Man
- Sermons for Hurting Hearts
- Miscellaneous Sermons – Volumes 1–5

Books

- Blueprints for Life
- How to Study the World's Greatest Book
- The Battle for God's Word
- Nine Steps to Backsliding

Daily Devotional and Online Paper

- Sign up for daily devotionals at www.oldpathsjournal.com

To Order These Products call
(304) 839-9531
or visit
www.oldpathsjournal.com
www.domelleministries.com